# *Dream*

# *Believe*

# *Achieve*

*A musical journey*

## *Richard Stephens*

### *My Autobiography*

*Dream, Believe, Achieve*

Published by Binnins Books

Printed by Biddles Ltd., of Kings Lynn, Norfolk.

ISBN 978-1-914408-37-3

A CIP catalogue record for this book is available from the British Library

This book is autobiographical.

*Dream, Believe, Achieve*

*To all those wonderful people who inspired me...*

*both living and dead...*

*Dream, Believe, Achieve*

*Pictured at the organ of St Mary's Church, Haverfordwest*

Richard Stephens, Hon FNCM BA(Hons)
FVCM(Hons)AVCM(Hons) AFNCollM FNFCM FGMS FCSO MNCM
ANCM FRSA ARCM CTVCM.,
*Organist, Pianist, Conductor, Teacher*

*Dream, Believe, Achieve*

*Foreword by RSM WO Mike Davies (RTD)*
*Former Mayor and Admiral of the Port of*
*Haverfordwest*

I have for over thirty years had the pleasure of knowing and marvelling at the author's stamina and ability to engage with, and help others in any way that he can, especially those interested in music, singing and choral work.

Whilst I am truly in awe of his musical talents, qualifications and National awards, it is not for me to catalogue them here as I feel sure that all will become apparent as ones reads through the narrative of his memoires, reflecting the life of Richard Stephens, Musical Director extraordinaire, or perhaps in truth, only half of his life so far as he has just reached fifty-one!

Thinking of Richard's 'giving nature' is where I want to come in with my own comments in this foreword, for I know that there will be quiet, unspoken of kindly deeds that only the recipients will know about, for in addition to the hundreds, possibly thousands of hours of many years that he has dedicated to setting up new choirs – men's, ladies, children's and mixed choirs, and going on to establish them on the Welsh, and further afield, choral circuits. In addition, he has trained budding musicians in readiness for when he has been head-hunted for the next project.

I feel it worthy here to mention, that in addition to the incalculable man hours spent in the musical world, Richard has pursued a full time, professional career in the National Health Service, whilst in tandem with an exhaustive lifestyle plays his part as husband, father, grandfather and family man with the same (if not more) zest, care, love and attention.

Richard Stephens has also served as Town Councillor and Deputy Mayor of Haverfordwest, and he has attracted a number of successes in his dealings for the betterment of the County Town of Haverfordwest, and with my own knowledge as a past Mayor myself, I have no hesitation in recommending this autobiography, and do so hope that those who buy it and read it, will appreciate, not only the effort gone into its production, but also the nature of the man who wrote it, and not only for his public works but also in salutation for the many private music/voice lessons that Richard has given, completely without cost to the students, who, for whatever reason could not afford the normal tuition fees.

*S. Mike Davies*

*Past Mayor and Admiral of the Port of Haverfordwest*
*Past Sheriff of the Town of Haverfordwest*
*Burgess of Haverfordwest*
*Career Regimental Sergeant Major*

## INTRODUCTION

I have never been a procrastinator, but there is always a first time for everything, and this was it. The writing of my autobiography – a life in Music, or as my dear wife suggested a title, *'Dream, Believe, Achieve.'* At first, I did think that the title was ill-advised, as I wanted to title the book *'I did it my way,'* which would have probably been far more apt for me and my personality, but it could also have been interpreted as somewhat immodest, and that is something I am not, nor was it something I wished to portray. Having said this, I have 'done it my way,' throughout my 41 years in music performance. There is no other way to do it, I have always been true to myself.

I have written and re-written parts of this book many times and thank goodness we are in the days of modern word-processing machines as I would have been a nightmare with a manual typewriter. I hasten to add that for many years I did have a manual typewriter, an *Imperial* was the make of it, and she was a beauty. I remember buying it from a chap in Jeffreyston. I then promoted myself to the use of an electric typewriter, and then to a HP laptop and now I use an apple MacBook pro, which is a whole new ball game in informatics technology. Anyway, I digress…

I decided to write this book in 2020, on the occasion of celebrating 40 years as a church organist, but with the advent of the deadly Corona Virus bringing this country of Great

Britain to its knees and indeed the whole world, it was put on hold, although I did write bits here and there, but I lacked the motivation to do a proper job of it, but now, here it is, and I hope that you enjoy the journey as much as I have enjoyed reminiscing and writing about it.

I must thank my long-standing friend, Mike Davies for such a wonderful foreword to this book. I have had the pleasure of knowing Mike since 1991when he became Mayor and Admiral of the Port of Haverfordwest. Mike worked tirelessly for the town and county and all its residents. I have never known such a human dynamo. He has ridden a bicycle along the banks of the river Nile, he has climbed mountains, run numerous marathons and walked thousands of miles for charity, and now, at the age of 83 he still does what he has always done so well. A man of military might, a Sandhurst instructor and a special forces soldier, Mike has done it all and seen much action. He and I are Burgesses of Haverfordwest, and there was nobody more deserving of this honour than he. Mike, I salute you dear friend, as does the whole population of Pembrokeshire for what you did for us all over so many years.

I also want to thank my dear late Grandmother, Hannah Davies, without whom this book would not be written. It was her influence that inspired me to begin learning the piano in 1975, becoming a chorister and then an organist, and she believed in my ability and was always a listening ear when I needed a moan and groan! She was somebody I could always approach with a problem or concern, and I would have direct, sound advice in return. She sadly left us in 2003, and I miss her every day, and 'thank you' will never be enough for the influence she had on my life. She was one of the best.

I must thank my dear wife, Gail. Not only for putting up with me for over 27 years, but for supporting all my ideas without question throughout all this time. She is not only my wife, but also my manager, and she offers me sound, solid advice, what to accept and what not to. I will ask her what to do about such and such, and whatever advice she gives I know that it's the best. She is simply the best.

This book is certainly not exhaustive by any means, because to be so would expand it to about 1,000 pages! Instead, it focuses on snippets of my musical life over the past 41 years, and I have imparted some of my thoughts on certain aspects of life along the way, or as I prefer to call them, 'observations.'

It's been somewhat difficult to write, because one must ensure that one stays the right side of libel law, and that has been difficult I can assure you! It is generally accepted that during our professional life we meet some prats, and I think I have met them all!! Being a musician and a person who is very exacting, I know my boundaries are small, and it doesn't take much for people to get on my nerves. Although some of what I am saying by means of an introduction is somewhat more detailed within the book, it is good to give a forewarning of what you are in for! I am not someone who suffers fools gladly, nor do I put up with anything under duress. I also firmly believe that quitting whilst ahead is key, and never allow your sell by date to pass, as people will only remember you for what you fail to do, not remember you for what you once did to bring pleasure and joy.

I do wish that I could have my life over again as there is so much I would do differently. With the knowledge, skill, and expertise I now have, coupled with my generous yet somewhat brusque nature, I would have been far more successful than I became. Hindsight is a wonderful thing, but of course, I believe that what is for us is meant to be, and there you have it dear friends. Thank you for buying my book, and now it is time to buckle up and enjoy the ride!!

## CHAPTER ONE
### *The beginning*

I was born in 1970, January the 27th to be exact, some 5 weeks premature, born by emergency Caesarean section at St Thomas' infirmary hospital in Haverfordwest, weighing in at a little over 5lbs. Certainly a lot has changed since then!

This book is, in the main, to celebrate and capture a little of my 41 years in music making but do forgive me for adding other little personal snippets along the way, to help you build a picture of what life was like, growing up and indeed as it is now in 2021, and the years in between.

The 1970s was, without doubt, one of the hardest decades from a socio-economic perspective. My parents and grandparents witnessed, during this decade, much recession, 3-day working week, power cuts with increased regularity, industrial action and so much more. So, I can only begin to imagine how difficult it must have been to bring up a new baby in these circumstances, and money was scarce. The generations gone before, including my generation it must be said, are a stoic lot, whereas the buttercups of today wouldn't be able to cope in such circumstances. I ought to warn you too, dear reader, not to expect political correctness within these pages. I do not subscribe to political correctness, although I would not go out of my way to offend anybody, but as the old saying goes, *'if the cap fits… wear it.'* In my humble opinion, 'PC' is the modern-day cancer that is killing this country bit by bit. Nobody can have an opinion nowadays without it offending some faction or minority group. It has become terribly sad that we must now live our lives in this way.

Growing up in the 1970s was generally good fun. Our neighbourhoods were safe, and everybody knew everybody. We were always given advice *'not to accept sweets from strangers,'* but we didn't really grasp the true meaning of that, but there were not the issues within society then as there is today, or they were certainly well hidden, and this is how it should have stayed. I was born into a loving and hard-working family, and for the first 10 years of my life we shared a large, Edwardian house with my grandparents. The family was very close, and I wanted for nothing. I was cared for beyond measure, and I will always be truly grateful to mum and dad and my grandparents for everything they did for me.

1975 was the year when my parents and grandparents thought I ought to do something musical. Learning the piano was almost a rite of passage in those days, and nearly all my contemporaries were doing the same thing. There was certainly an ideology of *'keeping up with the Joneses,'* and a degree of superciliousness surrounding the learning of a musical instrument. Sadly, this still exists today, especially if a pupil has a 'pushy parent,' and believe me, many do, and without wishing to seem sexist, it is usually the mother! I've met some 'battle-axes' during my teaching career I can tell you!! I guess it can be levelled at anything in life, but music, and in particular music performance can attract the divas, and the individual that is so far up their own posterior the daylight

13

has long disappeared. How unnecessary this is, and I have worked with many individuals like this over the years.

Almost all the kids in the small town that I grew up in had piano lessons, but it was a very small handful that made a success of it, and thankfully I was one of them. It wasn't easy, and I cannot say that I enjoyed my early experiences of music making. In fact, I hated it. There was no teaching style or learning style, every kid had to learn the same way, usually harshly, and there was no understanding of teaching styles being adapted to suite the individual student, so looking back we didn't have the easiest of experiences, and it was only the fittest survived the journey, those that I guess, had 'the gift.' Whitland, where I grew up, is a small market town in Carmarthenshire. I have always thought of it as a large village to be honest, and it was a close-knit neighbourhood, where everybody knew your business, and it they didn't they would make it their mission to find out. The old saying of *'common knowledge,'* is always worthy of my retort, *'common it may be, knowledge it is not,'* and I thank Peter Spence for that quotation. Despite some disadvantages, people had your back and watched out for you, and there was genuine care for each other, and there was a real respect, and we kids certainly respected our elders.

My parents, Hilary and Desmond Stephens are thankfully still on this mortal coil, and I am so appreciative as my father has suffered some awful cardiac problems, and in his early fifties, in fact, the age that I am now, he suffered cardiac arrest, and

14

received a quintuple cardiac by-pass graft at the University of Wales Hospital in Cardiff. That is approaching 30 years ago, and he is thankfully still going strong. Both my parents are self-sufficient, and I am thankful for their good health as they approach their 80s.

I ought to say at the outset that I was not an easy child. I was plagued with ill health throughout my childhood with perthes disease, which is a lack of blood supply to the acetabulum, or head of femur, causing it to become misshapen, which makes movement painful and difficult, and arthritis in later life. I suffer badly from arthritis in both hips now, and it causes me considerable pain. Sadly, playing the organ is not as comfortable as it used to be, but I will stick it out as it's not going to beat me! I was also very accident prone when I was young, having broken both arms, both wrists and legs. I was known personally in Glangwili A&E by Mr Harding-Jones, Dr Rees and his team. I spent many hours incarcerated in traction weights, as was the treatment in those days.

My first piano teacher was Mrs James, *Brondeg,* or Mrs *Harold* James as she was known. She was in fact Margaret, but everybody was known in those days by their husband's Christian name, or by their occupation. All welsh villages had a *Bentley 'the Milk',* or *Ernie 'the butcher,' Margaret 'the baker,' Ken 'the box'* (local undertaker) and so on. There was also a lovely lady who was known fondly as 'Big Ann,' and this prefix was because of her size, but can you imagine saying this today? Ann loved it, and nobody ever referenced her surname.

These sorts of colloquiums are endearing, and this practice is more prevalent in Wales than in any other country in the world, we are a strange breed, but like I said, it was never said in any way other than endearment.

I displayed musical prowess early on by sailing through the graded examinations of the London College of Music, gaining Merit and Honours at every stage. Even then it did come relatively easily to me, as I was not a great one for

practising the piano. I found it tedious and of little interest to be honest. The pieces were tuneless, the scales seemed like a total waste of time, and there was nothing to excite me.

My first experiences of a musical instrument, like many other children was the treble recorder in infant school. I have forgotten how many times a quick blast of '*three blind mice*' has helped me through my adult life! I could also play the glockenspiel, rather well I might add (two sticks), but I was never destined to be an Evelyn Glennie. I was destined for better, more powerful beasts, like the pipe organ, not hitting stupid little metal bars with wooden sticks with balls on the end! I was heading for the mighty 'King of Instruments,' and this is when my musical learning took on a whole new meaning, and my enjoyment soared.

In 1979 I was first introduced to the pipe organ as a 'player.' I had 'experienced' a pipe organ many times before, but never to actually 'have a go.' I found it intriguing how such an instrument, which essentially is a box of whistles, could create such wonderful sounds and demonstrate such power when required, and then reduce power so the sounds were infinitesimal.

My first experiences of large, powerful pipe organs were at Westminster abbey and the Royal Albert Hall, where the very seats you were sitting on would rattle your teeth in your head! It was awe-inspiring, and I knew at a young age that I wanted to sit at an organ and make the same noise!

However, my first experiences playing an organ was at St Mary's parish church in Whitland, which was a small, two-manual instrument with a small, flat pedal board with only a Bourdon 16', although it could be coupled with swell and great, which gave it a little extra boost. I always thought that it was the type of instrument that J.S. Bach himself would have played back in the 17th Century! However, to a 10-year-old, it was huge, and took some effort to control!

1979 was the year when I started to explore the possibility of playing the organ, or should I say, *learning to play* the organ. I cannot remember what grade I had achieved on the piano at this stage, but it was about grade 6. I started off by learning simple hymns, but playing them as you would on a piano, rather than the bass line being played by the feet as the pedals were too weak and insignificant.

I learned more and more hymns, and this is what rocketed my sight-reading ability. I always gained full marks for my sight-reading, and even now I usually play something at first sight, as practise time is just not available. I have a quick look through to check for any modulations or little figures that can catch one out, but that's about it. Sometimes I mark some pedalling in, but not usually. God gave me this ability because he must have known what a lazy learner I am. I really do believe that music within our soul is a gift, and this is what allows you to have immense enjoyment, and have notable success, which then brings about more enjoyment, and so the wheel turns…

My first official engagement as an organist was on the 24th of May 1980, when I played for a full wedding ceremony, complete with both marches as well as accompanying a local singer, Rosina Thomas, who performed '*The Wedding,*' by Joaquin Prieto, during the signing of the register. When I think about this now it was a huge ask of a 10-year-old, and a significant risk for the wedding couple to take. How many people would trust a 10-year-old to play the organ correctly for the most important day of their lives? I cannot remember if these services were captured on VHS or Cine film at that time, but even so, there was a huge responsibility on the shoulders of a whippersnapper!! However, despite being quite nervous, I carried it off brilliantly without any mistakes whatsoever. Richard Stephens had arrived, and the rest of the journey was going to be plain sailing – not! When I became more proficient and could use the pedals correctly, and this was probably about 1982, but if a particular passage was difficult, and the pedals were not really part of the musical structure of the piece, I would leave them out for a little, just so my brain could concentrate on playing the manuals correctly. It was a philosophy that worked for me. Thankfully now, I don't have to do this... well, not all the time, and holding a fellowship in organ performance, I shouldn't admit to it! I'm a lazy learner! I took it all in my stride, but to be able to do this at 10 years of age was something rather special.

I had played for some evening services prior to the wedding, but not before 1980. I remember my first hymn I learned was '*Glory be to Jesus,*' the hymn for Passiontide. I don't think it was Passiontide, but it might have been. Whitland church tended to have whatever hymns they liked as and when, there was no compunction to stick to the theme or the day. The second hymn I learned was '*Hail to the Lord's anointed,*' and following that, '*O God our help in ages past.*' I shudder to think how many times over 40 years have I now played these hymns; it must be several hundred times, or more. In my study nowadays I have about 17 hymnals, crammed with every conceivable hymn.

Learning a piano in the 1970s was, as I said earlier, was almost expected. Whitland had two main piano teachers – Mrs Harold James, ALCM., and Mrs Blethyn, ALCM., There was also Mrs Lorna Irving-Jones, LGSM., who was Head of Music at Narberth Secondary school, but she didn't have many pupils, or she was certainly not sharing the numbers of Mrs Blethyn, who taught most of the town. Mrs James was a close second.

Whitland was a divided town, into the Welsh and English-speaking contingents, and it was almost a case of *never the*

19

*twain shall meet.* The welsh-speaking contingent went to Chapel, so was taught by Mrs Blethyn, who was the principal organist at Tabernacle Chapel, whilst the English-speaking went to Church, and so to Mrs James. In the 1980s there was a lot of dissentions within the town, centred around the Hywel Dda memorial garden. It was taking away a very important connecting road and people were not happy. The welsh nationalists ploughed on regardless, and won the day, and the road was closed. However, the English-speaking people came back fighting and after a long battle, the road was reopened, and despite it being rather lovingly block paved, the road was once again introduced to traffic. During the public debates, of which there were many, opinions became very heated, and to be honest it created a bad atmosphere within the small community. The welsh nationalists tended to be somewhat narrow minded, and many of them were members of '*Cymdeithas yr iath Cymraeg*' and took to daubing English buildings and signs with paint. I like passion within a cause, but it was getting out of hand in all honesty. I like a bit of dulux matt, but not necessarily on the walls of public buildings, thrown like Rolf Harris had suffered some sort of frenzy; 'Can ya tell what it is yet? Um…no!' Each to their own, of course.

St Mary's Church in Whitland was 'low church' in tradition. A new vicar came on the scene in 1980 by the name of Revd Nigel Griffin, BA., He had served his curacy at St Peter's in Carmarthen, and he was new and fresh, and arrived with many ideas. Like all new brooms he swept clean, and he made himself incredibly popular in the town by frequenting all the drinking establishments and mixing with everybody. It was not long before he had people going to church like the Pied Piper of Hamlin! The Griffins were indeed a breath of fresh air to the parish, and we grew, both in number and in vision and activity. Our Sunday school was thriving as was the church choir. Nigel Griffin

was like (excuse the expression) *'cat's shit,'* he was everywhere, literally! I will tell you more later in the book.

I ought to mention at this point, that whilst this book is divided into chapters, some will be short and others will be long, so do go along with this. I did consider writing the book as a narrative, but I decided against it, because having chapters was easier for me to compartmentalise what I needed to write.

It's been lovely writing this book because as I have trawled through my memory; I have resurrected memories long hidden, and it brings me back to a very enjoyable period in my life, when time seemed to stand still, and the stresses of everyday life had not begun, and my word how I wished it had stayed that way!

## CHAPTER 2

*The church and me*

My family had worshipped at St Mary's in Whitland for many years, certainly since my grandparents married in the early 1940s.

St Mary's is a small (ish) church, situated along the banks of the river Taf, almost at the Pembrokeshire end of the town. I ought to point out that one half of the town is in Carmarthenshire and the other half in Pembrokeshire.

The church's seating capacity is about 150 at a push, and back in the 1980s it was often full. Generations of families had worshipped there, and it was a following of tradition by the generations which followed. Organised religion is just that in the main, tradition. How many people go to church or chapel today just because it is something they have always done and their parents before them? I would hazard a guess and say the vast majority. I must say, at this point, that for me, going to church is more than tradition, and indeed far more than playing the organ. It is an opportunity to explore our inner being and to be calm and contemplate, and I always look to feeling better coming out than I did going in. I always say that if religion works for the individual, then it is doing its job, and I certainly don't believe that thrusting it on other people bears fruit. It's important to me, and that's all that matters as far as I am concerned.

For me, certainly in my formative years, it was all about the music. Church and sacred music was awe-inspiring, and I felt a captivating need to be involved in it.

Other children who were the same age as me also 'had a go,' but failed miserably, in so much that when they played hymns, they were taken at such a slow pace, nobody would ever have been able to sing along to them. As I said earlier, at the age of 10, I was able to play a complete service, and I cannot overly recall being that terrified at the prospect. It was, in fact, something I looked forward to doing, and of

course, perspective is so different when one is young. To me, in 1980, the organ in St Mary's Church might well have been at Westminster Abbey as to the importance it held for me playing it. I was certainly doing a 'big pants' job, and that started my career of 41 years to date. Was it luck? I do wonder how much of it was luck, but I am not naturally a lucky person. In fact, if I was in a marching band, I would be the prat on a piano! Luck and I don't share a marriage made in heaven I can assure you. If somebody was given a bucket of Gold, mine would be a bucket of sh....! Yes, you've guessed it!

I don't think any of it was luck, but rather a mixture of hard work and having been given a wonderful gift. I showed great prowess very early on, and this isn't always something that is taught, or *can* be taught, it is all about natural proficiency, and an ability which comes from deep within your soul, and this was me. I had to practise, of course I did, but it flowed easily and very naturally. From that young age I took command of the organ and wasn't afraid to play it to its fullest potential. It really is a wonderful thing to feel totally comfortable with something, and for me it is playing the organ. Nowadays the moment I slide onto an organ stool, I am about to do something that brings myself and others immense joy, and what can rival this?

The resident organists at that time in St Mary's was Mrs Margaret Bevan, MA., Mrs Rowie James, LLCM(TD) ALCM., and Mrs Gaynor James, with Mrs Harold James, ALCM., being the coordinator of everything musical, and indeed non-musical!! (All churches have somebody like this) I remember badgering them to allow me to play some of their evening services for them, and they always agreed.

Rowie James always gave me £2 for playing her service, so she was my favourite! I was never in it for the money, but this was kind of her, but in the words of Tesco *'every little helps.'* I guess she was the one who most enjoyed a Sunday evening in front of the telly watching *'Bullseye.'*

Sadly, today's society has become more and more secular, and the importance of going to a place of worship isn't there in the grand scheme of things. The theology of religion has always been about the mystery, and we have bred a generation of people nowadays who must see something tangible to believe it. Our world and society have become greedy, everybody is so selfish and there is little love for a fellow human being anymore. Where did we go wrong? It all started in my opinion with Sunday trading laws, allowing shops to open on Sundays. In addition to this, the family unit is not so intact as it was in the 1970s. We hear of divorce today like we change our socks, but in the 1970s it was rare. Family units were the nurturing heart of the home, there was a mum and dad and usually the stable influence of grandparents too.

Drugs and drug abuse was something we never heard about, and the other little minority pastimes were also hidden. We now live in an *'anything goes'* society, and respect for anything, let alone religion, has all but gone. I am something of a traditionalist and proud of it, and whilst there were difficulties in years past, I still maintain that society was better off. There was certainly greater respect for our fellow human beings, pornography was confined to the top shelves, and child exploitation was never heard of. As society becomes more liberalised, so these evil pastimes rear their ugly heads, and modern life has made us somewhat immune to the ways of the world as they currently stand. You can read more of my soap box in the final chapters.

At 51 years of age, I long for a return to the values of the past. Technology has moved on and brought us a better experience in many ways, but at what cost? We now wait for nothing; we can shop 24hours a day, 7 days a week from our armchair. We can order food by pressing buttons on our mobile phones and it comes delivered shortly afterwards. We can now do everything 'online,' and I guess it has made us lazy as a nation. Sunday is no longer a day where people go to church, and many churches lost their choirs when sport activities took place on a Sunday, which I found particularly sad.

Very few people fought our corner; nobody stood up and said that this was wrong, as people who go to church or chapel are seen as some bygone relic, and by so doing, they allowed modern-day cancers to ruin this great country, and to ruin the much-needed family unit. I must say, whilst on the subject, *'political correctness'* is another reason that this country of ours is fast going down the pan. Nonsensical, idiotic rules and regulations of what you can and cannot say or do, 'gender neutral' and all that rubbish. It's no longer a *gingerbread man,* it must be a *gingerbread **person.*** To me, all of this is total poppycock, and it has no home in my being I can assure you. I am an ardent advocate of man and woman, of the family unit, decency for fellow human beings, and respect for age-old traditions which brought the best out in society.

Nowadays children are subjected to knowing an Uncle Margaret and Aunty Fred, as well as coping with all this gender-neutral rubbish! This country needs to 'grow a set of balls' and do away with such rubbish! As you can probably tell, I am *very* passionately against this baloney. If, however, people are stupid enough to believe in all this codswallop then good luck to them, people used to believe in the boogie man too, but it didn't get them very far, did it? I don't like to think of myself as very old-fashioned, but I have immense respect for the past traditions, and I guess by now you have already come to that conclusion!!

There are, however, occasions when I reminisce. I am always taking trips down 'memory lane,' and this is something I have always done. I have always said that my brain will be the death of me. I had (in 1991) a measured IQ of 148 and was eligible for MENSA membership, but didn't bother with that. I certainly didn't fit in with that loony lot, but I'm very much a thinker. In fact, I am an over-thinker in everything, and my brain never slows down or switches off, and it often causes me significant stress. Second best will not do for me, and if I was handwriting an A4 page, one little error and the whole page would be torn in two, and I would have to start again. I have OCP in certain things, and it drives me around the bend, but we are what we are. I guess that musicians are a peculiar breed, and whilst there is a lot about my personality I would change, there is a lot I am proud of too. What you see is what you get, and I am fiercely loyal to my loved ones and close friends.

My personality is one whereby I do not suffer fools gladly, and I have little time for 'small talk.' Having said this, however, I am always up for a laugh, a joke, and a prank or two, but when it comes to being serious and the need to be professional then I am it, without wavering. I have never had a large circle of friends, simply because I was not really doing things that endeared me to others of the same age. When I feel comfortable with somebody then we become friends, but this takes time. I am somewhat of a 'keep myself to myself' type, so would never have a large group of friends, but the ones I do have I am fiercely loyal to and vice versa, so I am very lucky. I guess I am an 'arm's length' type of person, and it really is only the chosen few that I feel comfortable being around.

My church life sometimes was a curse, in so much that I had to do a 'big pants' role from such a young age. I was a chorister, complete with ruff and starched surplice at the age of 5, and at the age of 10 was appointed a church organist, and at aged 15, a choir director!! Not your average pastimes for a teenager, certainly not nowadays. I also served on committees from the age of 15 and was the youngest PCC Secretary ever at the age of 18!! I have great administration skills, and in addition to music, this is also one of my gifts. I often think that church and sacred music was somewhat confining, and I did not experience many genres of music, but it was a genre that chose me I think, and music is such a huge subject area, that was my niche, and there I was to stay.

Whilst at high school I was often ridiculed for going to church and for playing the organ, but thankfully, I took most of it in my stride. High schools focused so much on sporty pupils that the more creative, arty pupil didn't stand a chance. PE teachers were quite frankly, prats in shell suits with a whistle around their necks, and I remember one occasion when a PE teacher poked fun at me in front of my class when I forgot my cross-country kit. She said that *if she could get a piano for me, I could go round the field on that!* What a horrible cow she was, and I never forgave her for that. Of course, everybody laughed, expect me. I didn't find it in the slightest funny. Revenge is always best served cold, and many moons later I went into a music shop in Carmarthen, and there was the very same woman, long retired, serving behind the counter. I pretended that I didn't recognise her, but I knew instantly who she was, and I also remembered what she had said to me all those years earlier. As I queued to pay for what I wanted, I could see her looking at me, trying to work out who I was. When it was my turn to pay, she asked me if I was 'Richard Stephens the musician?' When I said yes, she said, 'you don't remember me, do you?" I lied. I certainly did remember her. When she 'reminded' me of who she was, and she went on to say how 'well I had done,' I said calmly… *"You poked fun at me one day*

## Dream, Believe, Achieve

*Saying that I should go around the field on a piano. I have done exceptionally well as a musician, thank you, and here I see you are serving in a music shop. How the mighty hath fallen, goodbye."* I walked out of the shop, took a deep breath, and vowed never to go into that shop again. She was mortified and her gob hit the deck!! Result! I had waited 30 years plus to do that!

I was always picked on and ridiculed and called names for my church life. One day I felt the 'red mist' descend and I reacted harshly. I was 16 years of age by now, and enough was enough. The 'gobby little shite' wasn't quite so brave when he was minus his front teeth! It only took one punch to knock 4 teeth clean out of his head, and in fact, one tooth was buried into my knuckle! He crashed to the ground like a sack of spuds, and I had knocked him clean out. I was never proud of what I did, as I am not a fighting type, but there comes a limit within us all. It was never a fight; it was one hit. I could easily have killed him that day, and my strength and indeed temper frightened me. I will not put up with anybody being wronged in any way, and I will always defend harshly if needed. I always say that I am like a rattle snake, perfectly harmless if left to bask in the sunshine, but tread on me and I will react, and react harshly. From 1986 to this day, I have never allowed myself to be pushed around. As a teenager I had no confidence, and I hated social interaction, and yet I could play the organ without any issue, for any service, anywhere. It was where I felt comfortable and at home.

Church has always been my second home for the past 46 years, so it is part of who I am. It's one of the few things that I am good at, and where I consider myself "an expert," and there is no hierarchical nonsense where the more elevated the position, they more they **think** they know. I have reached the top of my tree, and I now enjoy swaying in the breeze!

Something changed that day amidst the aggression, in so much that the bullying days were done, and ever since then I will speak my mind, and I could not care less if the listener agrees or disagrees with what I am saying. My opinion is *always* my own, and that is very important to me, and I stick with it if I know it is right, although I am the first to apologise if I am wrong. I disliked school intensely, as I found it a total waste of time, and I *always* looked forward to church and the next sitting on the organ stool. School got in the way, and I don't think in the 1980s schools knew how to cater for the extremely musical pupil, but if you were sporty... the world would be your oyster! I must say that I also loved History, and I was extremely good at it too. I was academic but to me, my life was in church and on the organ stool! I somehow drifted along not having a clue as to what I would do with my life later. When I was in high school, I was accompanist to the school choir, and I played the piano for the morning assembly about 3 times a week. I remember the deputy Head and I wrote a song together, it was called, 'in the fullness of time,' he wrote the words and I the music. A photograph of me seated at the organ of St Davids Cathedral back in 1986 bedecked the 'wall of fame' at the school for many years after I left. Up until a few years ago it was still there!

Anyway, back to the story…

May 24th, 1980, is the day that I became an organist, taking my turn in the rota of three, but also beseeching my colleagues to play for more and more of their Sundays, to which they agreed. I always achieved 100% in my sight-reading at examination, simply because I had such a lot of music to learn in a short space of time, so it helped enormously. In fact, I had to learn 4 new hymns every week, as well as a chant. I also had to play music at a drop of a hat for the school choir. It's always poor practice for students purely to stick to examination music at the expense of all other.

In 1985 I was asked to join the St Clears deanery music committee. How many 15-year-olds do this? It scares me sometimes to think how much excitement I had?! I felt comfortable around adults, and I could always speak their language and interact of their level, so it felt natural. The chair of the committee was the then Rural Dean. He certainly was not my favourite person and there was '*something of the night*' about him. He was always grinning like a 'Cheshire cat,' and I was once told, never trust somebody who smiles too much! The other members of the committee were Revd Alun Howells, BA., FRCO LTCL LLCM., who was the Vicar of Meidrim, and deanery organist. He was a fine player, but deaf, and as such played loudly most of the time. He was a character, and I thoroughly enjoyed our chats. He loved a 'wee dram' and always smelt like a distillery, but it was what made him who he was. An educated chap and musically brilliant too, and as far as I knew he was much loved as a parish priest.

Everybody thought the world of Alun, and as a bachelor, the women of the parish looked after him very well and fed him most days, and of course, he lapped it up.

The director of Music was Mrs Elizabeth Jameson, a lovely woman who was very kind to everybody. She wasn't the greatest of musicians, but her manner was such that she made you look forward to going to rehearsals.

My role was assistant organist, and I often played for deanery choir rehearsals, usually held in either St Martin's, Laugharne; St Mary's in St Clears or Meidrim Church. I remember playing Beethoven's '*Creation hymn*' for the deanery choir to sing in procession at Laugharne church, it was a tingling moment. Revd Alun built a pipe organ in the vicarage from scratch, every bit of which he made himself and installed. He had to have it tuned professionally as he couldn't hear it properly to make out the hertz.

He gave me great advice as to how to tackle Bach's pedalling as at that time I always found Bach's music terribly unforgiving to play. In fact, even now, the music of J.S.Bach demands an ability like none other, perhaps with the exception of the French school, the likes of Widor and Gigout. It is very complex music, containing complicated counterpoint. I do play quite a lot of Bach's music, but I always play what I know well. Bach's music is not something one can just pick up and play; it will catch out even the most seasoned of organists. The man was a genius, and I will only ever play Bach after a long spell of practise. I have my favourite few preludes, fugues, and toccatas and that's it. I try to avoid it if I can!

The Sunday school festivals were the highlight of the year. They took place every May/June, at either St Mary Magdalen in St Clears, or St Martin's in Laugharne. These were the two largest churches in the deanery, and two with the finest organs too. I thoroughly enjoyed the festivals, and they were wonderful events to facilitate fellowship between churches. There is a tendency for churches to become insular, and fiercely independent of each other, but we all love church for the same reasons, so it is good to come together. It's a great shame that such festivals cease to exist nowadays. I will have to lobby for them to come back in some shape or form.

My mother's side of the family hail from Laugharne, so this is always somewhere I have felt quite at home. The corporation of Laugharne is a hard nut to crack, and in those days, one had to be 'accepted,' or be viewed with much suspicion. As soon as they knew I was 'Hannah's boy' from Rectory farm, I was one of them and never looked back. I sat in the bass section next to the late Manny Francis, who was a stalwart of St Martin's church choir. I remember him with fondness, and he always used a magnifying glass! It was quite funny to be fair. The choir at St Martin's Laugharne were quite proficient as choirs go, and I remember my grandmother telling me stories of days gone by when Mr E.V. Williams was the choirmaster, and when the choir numbered 30 plus, and sang 'big sings' as I call them. I remember one of my teachers at school, Mr Jeff Watts, and he could be a tyrant to say the least, who was a long-standing member of the Laugharne church choir. In 1990 I directed a singing day at Laugharne Church, and Mr Watts was in the choir. The roles had turned, and I made sure he paid attention and was sitting up straight. How we laughed about that. He was a good old stick really.

Mrs *Harold* James, my first piano teacher, died in 1983, very suddenly, and I owe her a great debt of gratitude. She could make me cry and did so often, but she believed in me. I was very touched when she died because I was approached shortly afterwards by her sister to say that Mrs James wanted me to have first choice at any of her music books. I still have hymn books and other church music books belonging to Mrs James dating from the 1920s, and they are in excellent. condition. I was also requested to play the organ at her funeral, and this was quite an honour, and I was 13 years old at the time. After Mrs James' death, I had piano tuition with Pat Jones, B.Mus., ARCM., who was head of Music at Trinity College.

I have entitled this chapter '*The church and me,*' but there is so many different things about *the church and me* that I can put in here, so I will end this chapter with some generic things and come back to church career in later chapters.

We all need to feel comfortable in life with whatever it is we do, and church is always somewhere I have been comfortable. As I said earlier, I suffered terribly in my younger years with a sort of inferiority complex, and my 'hobby' if you like has turned my life around in so many
ways. I had little confidence, I hated leaving home, and enjoyed silence and quiet times. Playing the church organ changed most of this and really changed me. Music changed me, and I am very grateful for that. I would have made a

success of being away at a choir school if were not for the fact that home is where the heart is!

I have never been somebody that seeks the limelight, although over the years I have stupidly been thrust into it by not making the right decision, but I guess it's part of life, and what doesn't kill us makes us stronger, or so we hope. We all take a wrong turn on the road of life, and perhaps some change our destiny, but it's all about human frailty, and learning from where we went wrong, and what we could have done differently. Smashing that lad's teeth out was not a proud moment after the mist cleared, but it did make me a bit of a hero in school for all 5 minutes, but I was seen in a different light for the wrong reasons for quite some time afterwards. I did regret that incident.

As I have become older, I now have much more confidence, and can 'work a room' as good as anybody. I can conduct choirs of several hundred people, talk in front of hundreds, so the days of the 'old Stephens' have long gone, and good riddance too. Having said this, however, I still appreciate calmness and times of quiet, because it is in these moments that we reflect and take stock of our lives. Time is precious and our lives are hectic. It is good to take time out of the 'rat race,' sit and think, listen to soothing music, and allow it to transport you through time and space, to a memory long hidden, to enable you to walk with loved ones long gone, the possibilities of inner calm are endless. As I get older, I appreciate this more and more. My study at home is my sanctuary, it is where I can shut the door on the outside world, and within its walls is everything musical, the books I have written, and about another 300 besides, and about 1,000 music books and pieces. It's quite simply my very much-loved *man cave* and indeed my 'happy place.' I think we all need a haven where we can remove ourselves from the world now and again. In my study I am taken to wherever I want to go, whether it is listening to colleagues singing on the CD of Westminster Abbey at Christmas time, or Karl Jenkins' *the Armed man.* Equally, I like a bit of '*Ernie*' by Benny Hill. My musical taste, despite being brought up on Anglican chant, hymns, anthems, and descants, is very eclectic! I also loved going with Gail to the o2 arena to see *Westlife* live, and I can bop along like a good 'un, as they say in Pembrokeshire!

Church Music will always be my life, and I have found my spiritual home now in St Katharine and St Peter's Church in Milford Haven. I will go into more detail further into the book, but from the moment I walked through those west doors, I received a warm, genuine welcome, and they are such a lovely group of people. They really are a church family in every sense of the word. God bless them, everyone.

Going back to the early 1980s, and it was a time when my hearing ability began to deteriorate. I suffered measles very severely as a child. In fact, I was almost hospitalised, but when I recovered, it had damaged my hearing significantly. I had ENT surgery at Glangwili Hospital in Carmarthen, and Mr '*slasher*' Morgan, the ENT Surgeon, inserted 'grommets' on several occasions, which aimed to drain the 'glue ear' from the middle ear. They were not overly successful, and over time, the surgery has left scarring on my ear drums, which affected my hearing greatly. It did impact on my life, not overly the music, but my interaction with people. I often misheard what was being said, and not having the confidence to ask them to repeat themselves many times, and as for noisy environments, I avoided them like the plague. I also had tonsils and adenoids removed, as well as an operation on the middle ear, all at the same time. I was hospitalised for almost 2 weeks! I was never allowed to swim as I couldn't get water in my ears!

My hearing deteriorated so much by 2006, that I became the wearer of two hearing aids, and this helped massively, although they took a considerable period to become accustomed to, and there would be periods when I wouldn't wear them as they were uncomfortable and difficult to use in conjunction with the telephone etc. Over the years that followed, my hearing deteriorated further, and in theatres and concerts I now must rely on their telecoil or loop system to be able to hear the performers on stage. I find the loop system frustrating because in churches etc, they are not used correctly so therefore, the hearing aid wearer suffers considerably.

I know my hearing, or lack of it, in recent years made my choral directing somewhat hazardous shall we say, because I was increasingly missing errors within sections, and it became somewhat embarrasing. This is one of the reasons that I have curtailed the majority of my choral directing. As I head into 2021 and beyond, my hearing aids' amplification is being increased, and my hearing deteriorates further. The prognosis for my left ear is not good, and the right side isn't much better, but hey-ho, I'm 'above ground,' and I am thankful for that. Hearing aids took a bit of getting used to from an aesthetic point of view, as it really made me feel somewhat 'disabled,' but I guess they are just like wearing glasses. Anyway, I cannot manage now without them, and it makes for a far more superior experience when listening to music. It really does take a lot to make me descend into doldrums, but my loss of hearing was one such thing that did.

From about 1985, every Saturday night I would stay with my grandmother and go to church with her at 8am on the Sunday. This was a said communion, but it was a way of me keeping her safe as she got older, and company too by being with her every Saturday night. I remember with much fondness, my ideal Saturday night was watching 'Dukes of Hazzard' on TV and having lovely Findus Crispy pancakes. For many years I attended church 3 times on a Sunday, and it was wonderful for me, and I have never regretted my life choices, and although I wasn't going out on a Saturday night to get sloshed like my mates, I was getting fulfilment in a different way, a way more suited to my personality as it was then. My night out was on a Thursday when I attended choir rehearsal, and I enjoyed several ciders, and many a night I would 'float' home about 11.30pm, and wake the dog in the process, and then my parents! Happy days.

## CHAPTER 3

*Opportunity Knocked*

In 1986 I was in Carmarthen on a Saturday, and I walked into St Peter's Church at the end of King Street. I was immediately transfixed by the organ playing, and when I stopped and listened closely, it was being played very efficiently.

Upon further investigation I could see a silver-haired lady sitting at a detached console of a rather fine pipe organ, playing a Bach Prelude and Fugue.

At the end of the part she was playing, we got chatting and of course it was all about the organ in general. She let me 'have a go,' on the organ, and thankfully in her book of BACH was a piece I knew well, so I played it. She was very impressed indeed and lost no time in telling me that the church was looking to appoint an organ scholar. This was music to my ears because I am, by nature, very ambitious (to a point).

This post would come with organ tuition from the organist, who I found out was Mrs Alice Male, ARCO FLCM., and she had been associated with Manchester Cathedral for several years before relocating to Carmarthenshire. In addition, Dr Michael Smith, D.Mus. FRCO (CHM), the Organist at Llandaff Cathedral was to provide tuition directly for me being organ scholar at St Peter's, it was part of the 'package' as it were.

I met with the vicar, Revd Canon Kerry Goulstone who was quite a fussy, eccentric character, clearly highly strung. He was very encouraging to me, and I accepted the two-year position.

I couldn't drive a car, so I had to rely on my father to take me to and fro, but he's the best dad in the world and never complained. I had to negotiate a bit of a re-jiggle as far as Whitland church was concerned, and St Peter's church officialdom allowed me to play for every evening service on a Sunday, which allowed me to remain in Whitland, playing for the morning service only. St Mary's was lucky to have other organists, so this plan was easily workable.

Being the organ scholar of such a large parish church with a fine musical tradition was the nearest thing to Westminster Abbey I was going to get in the diocese, certainly in a church. In fact, the standard was then, at that time, even was better than the standard of our Cathedral at St Davids, certainly at that time. The SATB choir at St Peter's was very proficient, and when I wasn't playing the organ, I would sing bass in the choir, and this is when I met Arwyn Price, and that started a long friendship between us. Arwyn served for many years on the West Wales committee of the RSCM., and we appeared as 'guest choristers' with many a church choir which deputised for cathedral choirs. The choir had many good singers, and one was the vicar's daughter, Brigette. She and I were good friends, and she really was a lovely soprano, and in 1986 she was my page turner at an organ performance at St Davids Cathedral.

My organ tuition went swimmingly with Alice Male and Dr Smith, gaining Grade 8 with distinction in the spring of 1986. In fact, I only lost 1 mark!! I won a high-achiever medal. Both were tough, and they had very high expectations from me, and it was my duty to deliver.

At the end of the two-year period, I was called to the vicarage for a meeting with Canon Goulstone. He was hugely grateful and wonderfully impressed with what I had been able to bring to his church, and what he offered me next certainly bowled me over. He offered me a full-time position of assistant organist at £3,000 per year, plus fees, plus the ability to use the organ to give lessons if I wanted to. This was a great opportunity, and at that time being a Cathedral organist was what I was aspiring to become, so this appointment would have been a great addition to my CV!

I agreed to the position, and everybody was happy. I looked forward with much anticipation to playing more and more and becoming part of the musical 'officialdom' of one of the leading civic churches in Wales.

After agreeing verbally to Canon Goulstone, I had the next hurdle to overcome, and that was breaking the news in Whitland. I knew only too well how it would be received, and it would not be good! I was correct, as it went down like a ton of bricks!

Throughout my musical career I have had to fight to convince people of the benefit of opportunities, but the blinkered loyalty to St Mary's Church was perhaps, in this instance, a little too considerable. I am not going to condemn my mother or grandmother for their stance because now a parent and grandparent myself, we don't always give the right advice, and as the adage says, *there is no good crying over spilt milk.* In life we miss many opportunities, and maybe there is a reason.

I was absolutely determined that I was accepting the opportunity as I am very focused and driven when I feel the need, especially when I was younger. If I wanted something I was going to achieve it. I was due to give Canon Goulstone my decision the following week, and I was looking forward to the meeting. I caught the train to Carmarthen, and I made my appointment bang on the nail as arranged.

The welcome I received when he opened the door was somewhat different, there was a slight cool breeze shall I say. When we reached his study and I accepted his offer to sit down, he told me that there had been developments. The 'development' was that Revd Nigel Griffin had contacted him and tore him off a strip for trying to 'poach his organist,' and as such, he thought it better if the offer be withdrawn. I could scarcely believe what I was hearing, and to be denied an opportunity such as this was contemptuous in the extreme. I did, in fact, ask Canon Goulstone to reconsider as I dearly wanted this opportunity, and I know he was greatly disappointed, but there was no wavering him. He did tell me, however, that Revd Nigel Griffin had been very much out of order in the way he had spoken to him, and they did not end the telephone call on very good terms. It was at that moment a spark within my musical soul was extinguished for St Mary's in Whitland, and I would have resigned there and then if it were not for the fact that I loved playing the organ and it was the only opportunity I was now going to get. I did explore the idea of various organ scholarships, but the money was a pittance, and not even enough for me to run a car when I was due to get one shortly. It is surprising how inadequate the basic salary is in a Cathedral, far less than I am earning now. I investigated the post of assistant organist at York Minster recently, and it was a little over £12,000 a year, plus fees. The 'fees' always make me laugh, as they are not guaranteed per se.

As I mentioned earlier, I am not known for having terribly good luck, and in August 1986, Whitland and surrounding areas were subject to wide and savage flooding. Inside our house the water rose about 3 feet up the walls, and in the streets, it was even deeper, just over 4 foot. I had bought a car ready for my 17th birthday, a lovely triumph dolomite 1.6 SE. My parents owned the car from brand new and then sold it to a next-door neighbour who had only done 1,000 miles in it. Sadly, when the pandemonium broke out as the flood waters rose, I got the keys to move the car to higher ground (I was driving on private land, so no offence was committed!) but I tripped in our garden on the way to the garage where the car was being stored and I lost the keys, not to be retrieved until the flood waters subsided and the car was ruined. During my years at home with my parents I didn't display any of my music certificates, they were in cupboards, and certainly not framed. I guess it was because I didn't have a music room, my piano was on the first-floor landing outside the bathroom! In the flood I lost them, save for one or two. In recent times I have had them replaced thankfully, and my 'wall of fame' in my study is something to be proud of, and even at my age I show them off, and make no apologies for it!

I couldn't bring myself to resign from St Mary's as I had too much to lose, but I did resign as choirmaster. I hated the job anyway, and this was the perfect opportunity to screw the vicar's plans, as he now was the only person available to take the choir. He was welcome to it. He did bring in Lorna Irving-Jones from time to time, but she was of chapel tradition, so she didn't have a clue of Anglican repertoire, which we know as liturgy. It wasn't a match made in heaven and she soon gave up too, although I was told that Rev Nigel and she were 'close' at one time. Griffin worked with the choir, and I was more than happy to take my turn accompanying them, but I never felt the same for Nigel Griffin from that moment on. He was seen as a disingenuous individual who betrayed me beyond measure, and I will never forget this. Having grown wiser in older age, I realise that he didn't want to lose me, but he ought to have talked to me about it and seen how the opportunity would have been good for me.

One of the greatest problems with working in the field of church music is that there is little disparity between the professional and the amateur organist. As long as a bum is on the organ stool for every service, there is little care as to the standard of musicianship that emanates from the player. This is something I have often struggled with. In some 'country-bumpkin' parishes, where time stands still and expectations are low, the parishioners and indeed clergy could not care less if an old doddery lady of 90 is scraping her way through a hymn, or whether the organist is a professionally trained musician, and in the grand scheme of things does it really matter I wonder? To me it does, but I suppose it could be questioned as if it really matters when glorifying God, and I often question why I have spent over £26,000 in tuition and examination fees since 1975, to compared in the same breath as aunty flossy who cannot play very well at all. I do generalise of course as many churches value greatly the benefits of having an adequate organist. It doesn't even have to be an organist in the real sense of the word, but a proficient piano player who is playing the organ would suffice. I can appreciate that I may seem somewhat sanctimonious here, but I firmly believe that the quality of worship offered to the glory of God **must** be the best possible. The old Pembrokeshire saying, 'it'll do,' in fact **doesn't** *do* for me, and I make no apology for that. Standards in everything must be high, and I have always set myself very high goals, many of which I have failed to achieve, but the majority I have, so that's all I can ask for, I guess. Sadly, we organists do get taken for granted, and all too often in life familiarity breeds contempt. I don't like being taken for granted because this is when a rot can set in. I like to stay fresh, and always bring something new to the listener's ear, so they too can stay fresh within my music.

The ideologies of the small quaint towns and villages has not evolved for many years, and the people are happy to live in the 'status quo' where nothing changes. Nothing moves forward, everything stays the same… forever and ever shall be, Amen! This school of thought is all very well, but there is always brighter and better to be had if we are prepared to work for it, but having said this, sometimes it is just good to go with the flow as it were, wo whatever floats your boat!

The opportunity to study at university was not denied to me, I had no intention of going. None of my contemporaries went to university, as in the 1980s it was mostly about apprenticeships. Going to 'uni' nowadays is something done by almost all 18-year-olds, regardless of grades and regardless of what they want to do. Degrees are now dished out like sweets, 2$^{nd}$ and 3$^{rd}$ class degrees which are no good to man nor beast. The world and his wife now get 'masters,' and back in the day, only a very few people ever had a master's degree. My parents certainly didn't have the money to send me to any swanky university, but even if they were millionaires, the concept would not have been attractive to me. I didn't like being away from home, so therefore a life as a chorister in Westminster Abbey into my early teens was not for me! (Too snobby for a 'Taffy' from West Wales). My late grandmother studied her SRN in nursing, as did so many others, but nowadays nurses have degrees. Is the care any better? I will leave you judge that one, but there really is no substitute for experience.

I undertook a performance course with the Royal College of Music, studying to become an associate (ARCM) a qualification that is now debunked and replaced many years ago, by the LRSM., I worked incredibly hard to achieve it, and for me at that time, it was more conducive than studying in a small poky room, miles from home. I did study for a university degree, but I 'worked from home' as it were, curtesy of the Open University. In 1988 I enrolled on a BA (Hons) degree course, studying humanities, with music main and modern history. My degree study lasted until early 1995, and I have to say that I have never worked so hard! There were many nights of study when I started at dusk and worked through until dawn. My TMA's were flying in, and I had some lovely tutors, who gave very sound advice. I even remember one of the popular music songs that I had to study, *Ghost town* by the *specials*. I had to analyse orchestral scores until they were coming out of my ears and writing projects. However, I achieved first class, but now, almost 30 years on, I have forgotten more than I learned, but I guess we are all guilty of that. Studying with the open university is far more difficult that attending a campus, simply because one must juggle the same amount of work, and study alongside whatever else you are doing in life, and for my second and third levels of the degree, my life was not in a good place. I would go night after night without sleep, and it took its toll, but it was worth it in the end. Was I sorry I didn't go to university the conventional way, not one bit! I could think of nothing worse.

I also applied, after much procrastinating, for an organ scholarship at Salisbury Cathedral but was pipped to the post on that one, but it was not meant to be. Don't you just hate that silly phrase? Of course, it was *meant to be,* I just didn't bloody get it! I can accept defeat graciously; I always shrug my shoulders and move on. Having said this though, as I have got older, and hopefully wiser, I do now think that things *are* or *are not* meant to be, for whatever reason as part of our destiny. Anything that involved moving away was always thought of as a half-hearted effort, and it's a terrible thing when one is plagued by an anti-social streak, although thankfully that has long gone! My next step in my life will be retirement, and I most certainly will not procrastinate over that, because that cannot come soon enough.

Thankfully having studied piano, conducting and organ through to fellowship level I have not failed a single examination. Sometimes maybe more by luck than judgment, but I did it. I did 'scrape' through one or two grades on the piano, but it really was simply that I didn't prepare as I ought. I guess that's life, but a pass is a pass I guess, and I was happy with that; I had nothing to prove to anybody only myself. I have never been guilty of doing something purely for kudos, I have always done things because I want to, I enjoy doing whatever it is, and the fulfilment I get out of it.
I personally couldn't care less what others think, nor could I care less about 'kudos.' I do everything because I enjoy it, and when I stop enjoying it, I don't do it. It really is as simple as that, and I know life is in shades of grey, but I am very much back and white. A foolish philosophy? Maybe, be we are all different, and that is to be celebrated. I could never do anything that I didn't enjoy, it really is against my religion!

In more recent times opportunities have been denied to me by people being jealous and working covertly to upturn my apple cart. People I regarded as friends, stealing my ideas, stealing my opportunities by undercutting me, and being a Judas, and when they are disguised as your friend, they are very difficult to spot.

*Dream, Believe, Achieve*

I will tell you about a whopper when you come to the chapter *'The national stage,'* so do look forward to that.

Please excuse the Americanism, but there is always somebody to *'piss on your parade,'* and we go through life keeping an eye out for such people, because they are not instantly recognisable simply due to their covert nature and sly ways, and like I said a moment ago, they are often in disguise as a friend, or perhaps a colleague. Yes, sadly I have had more than my fair share of people stealing opportunities for one reason and another, but by nature I'm not a grudge holder because I do believe in forgiveness from the heart. Even the worst people can deserve forgiveness, although sometimes it is very difficult, and even when forgiveness has been given, it is difficult, if not impossible to forget. I am sure that we can all recall events in our lives that we denied to us wrongly, and how it made us feel at that time? The important thing is that we dust ourselves down, stand up tall and get on with it. Always remember one thing, if in whatever walk of life, you find yourself, whatever your occupation, there will be individuals ready to trip you up, and it is simply because of *your* success, *your* ability, because deep down they want to *be* you; remember that. Jealousy is an all-consuming evil that eats away at everything that is good. I do not have a jealous bone within me, and it matters not who has what because I am wholly content with my lot, and proud of it. Yes, there are things I would have approached differently, but hindsight is always a wise kid. I was once told by somebody that jealous people envy you; bloody hell, don't bother do that, you'd be disappointed 'LOL.' I guess too that because I enjoyed great success so young, people do become jealous, and I even experienced 'jealousy vibes' from parents of contemporaries learning the piano because they didn't have the opportunity to play the organ in Church. One or two were quite vindictive, but why were they like this towards me? I was working hard to make a success of it, and I wasn't doing it simply to make my contemporaries look stupid or any less favoured than I. Some of them did try, but were never any good, and not once did I poke fun at them, but rather I gave them encouragement and really tried hard to work with them.

Who was the fool? The saying, 'you reap what you sow' doesn't always ring true. I have never done anything to promote *me.* I have done things because it is what gives me satisfaction. I am more than happy at home, but if an opportunity comes for me to do what I love, then I can always do it.

On a slightly different 'theme,' I want to tell you about another strong vocation I had which basically manifested itself in 2003, although I had similar thoughts as far back as 1988. In 2003, I felt that I should explore ministry, and look to the ordained ministry. It was horrendously tough, and I have to say it was not an experience I enjoyed. First of all, everybody I spoke to shrugged it off, and by now I was 'typecast' as an organist, and nobody within the church officialdom took me seriously as potentially anything else. The former Archdeacon of St Davids, the Ven Dennis Wight B.Th., did take me seriously, and it meant me coming away from the organ for a time for the main Sunday services and to explore my vocation through a process of discernment, with the Revd Canon Geoffrey Gwyther in Prendergast, who I knew well. I had finished my residency at St Martin's Church, and whilst still maintaining a freelance organist basis here and there where and when I could, my worshipping life was fully integrated at St David's Prendergast, as part of the discernment process. It was very, very tough to move away from the organ stool, and equally tough to be taken seriously working on the inner side of the communion rail.

I trained as a worship leader and as such I was able to take 'word' services, which I did quite regularly in Prendergast and at St James' Dale, where Dennis was the incumbent. The discernment process was tough and all-consuming, and certainly tested everything to the brink. I went to meet the Bishop, Rt Revd Carl Cooper, and this was again and interview full of questioning centered around my organ playing. I felt it somewhat unfair and intimidating if I am honest, as plenty of vicars were once (and still are) organists, such as Revd Canon Andrew Grace, B.Mus., FRCO., who is now rector of Tenby, and of course there is the Rt Revd Dr Richard Fenwick, who is an outstanding organist, as is Most Revd John Davies, former Archbishop of Wales. I wonder did these people have the same degree of interrogation.

I was also questioned up hill and down dale about the breakdown of my first marriage, and it was portrayed to me in such a way that we had to justify it all to the bench of Bishops. It did upset me because I had a church pedigree that was proven right back to 1975, and I know of ordinands who only found faith a few years ago!! I told you about my luck earlier!! Here it was manifesting itself once again!

Of course, adding insult to injury, Carl Cooper was later found out to be famously 'overly-friendly' shall we say with a female colleague, so who the hell was he to question me?! 'Tatty bye' as Ken Dodd once said. They didn't think me worthy, so it's their loss. I did start to explore the possibility again in 2020, but my requirement is more on the organ stool than in the pulpit, so I will now put the idea to bed. I failed to convince the so-called experts that it was a serious discernment, and I was only every considered an organist. To go forward with the process now would mean that I could no longer be the organist in St Katharine's Church, and this is not an option, as I could not leave them without anybody, and I very much enjoy my being there.

However, it doesn't matter because I can now concentrate on what I am good at, but I shall always wonder 'what if,' and wonder as to how some of the current day vicars actually made it through, as it beggars belief in some cases.

I really do believe that it is in the same in whatever occupation of professional life you lead. If you are good, and if you are anxious to seek better, then people above you put the blockers on it, pour cold water over your ideas, and generally keep you in such a place as to not ruin their fiefdom by diluting it with somebody with ability.

All too often in life you see the useless individuals getting promoted, and the reason is because they are not seen as a threat to those above them. The bright, keen, and challenging individuals are kept down where they are. It is a shame, and human nature, at times can be a pig! I really would throw some under a bus if I could get away with it!

I also firmly believe that if you are good at what you do, you are stuck with it, as the powers that be are reluctant to have you replaced. They think of themselves rather than allowing you to spread your wings and fly. I have experienced this time and time again, and I find it very frustrating, but I guess one learns to live with it after a while.

There is a saying of being a 'victim of your own success,' and to a degree this is very true. When you are good at what you do you can become indispensable, and people really don't want to lose you. I would stick my neck out to say that perhaps good organists really are indispensable!

I guess that we have all been denied opportunities at one time or another, and at the time it cuts deep, but perhaps they were not part of the greater plan for us? Who knows? Not only have I had opportunities denied to me, I must take some of the blame on myself simply because my personality is not a pushy one, so I am not one for promoting myself, and I guess by being modest one can lose out such a lot, but I'd rather be remembered for being modest and endearing rather than being a hugely successful bigot. There is a thought in life that being a gentleman is the best philosophy, and perhaps in years gone by that is perfectly true, but I am not too sure if gentlemanly manners and reticence bear fruit in the long term, because when we look at successful individuals, many of them have something of an 'over-bearing' personality shall I say...

## *Dream, Believe, Achieve*

Life is too short for many regrets, but I do have several, although I try not to let them cloud my life, because there is nothing I can do to turn things around now. Opportunities knocked for me in many different ways through the years, and for far too many inexplicable reasons they were denied to me, and I also too denied several offers simply because I had no intention of moving away. If I did, then I would not have the wonderful family that I have now, so it depends very much on perspective, doesn't it? As I have said elsewhere in this book, I firmly believe that our lives are mapped out for us well in advance, both the good, bad and indifferent, and we must embrace our opportunities, and not regret those opportunities we chose not to take, because at the time it seemed like a good idea to reject them.

As I have mentioned several times in this book, as a teenager I lacked such a lot of confidence, but in 1986 all of that changed for the better, not simply by attacking my nemesis after school, but attending a youth residential pilgrimage at St Davids for a week in August of that year. It was a week of fun, fellowship, music, workshops, exploring prayer through the music of Taize, and that week I changed for the better. Leading up to it I didn't want to go, but during that week I was also going to be the organist at the Cathedral for several occasions, and this was the huge attraction for me. I met some wonderful people that week who made a lasting impression on me it has to be said, and in my group was Dorrien Davies, prior to his training for the priesthood, and now he is the Archdeacon of St Davids. And also Sian Jones, who later went on to become Rector of Llanelli. It really was a week that changed me forever.

54

## CHAPTER 4

*St Peter's Church, Goodwick*

*&*

*Haverfordwest Ladies' Choir*

My appointment as organist at St Peters church in Goodwick, came somewhat out of the blue, following an in-depth conversation with the vicar of the parish at the time, the Reverend Stephen Thatcher. I will tell you all shortly, but first...

In the spring months of 1991, I decided that I wanted to form a choir with a difference. I did some art of an in-depth feasibility study and of course Pembrokeshire saturated with choirs, particularly male voice choirs, and the only ladies' choir that existed was at Neyland. This gave me an idea, to form a female voice choir with a difference. The difference being that I would try and attract slightly younger element, therefore creating a more youthful sound. Sadly, that was not to be although the choir had several younger members, but it was in the end a consistency of both young and old, and it worked well.

However, to enable the marketing machine to recruit members to this new venture was put into full swing and part of the adventure was the publication of posters to be distributed around the County, particularly in churches and in chapels. The reason I decided to display recruitment posters in such places, was because this was the sort of environment where they would be in all probability, and nucleus of singers.

One of the churches that I stopped at to display a poster in the church porch was St Peters in Goodwick.

Unfortunately, by the time I returned home several hours later, I received a telephone call from the vicar of the parish, Revd Stephen Thatcher, and he was not a happy chappie. He did not think it a good idea for secular posters to be displayed in places such as a church porch. To be honest with you I had never heard such gobbledygook in all my life. My thinking during that phone call was quite simply, no wonder these places are empty with ******** like this out the front.

When I took great pains to point out that I was not a secular person but already had quite a pedigree as a church goer, his attitude changed for the better, and in fact we had quite a meaningful conversation following that. He discussed the music with me, and it was clear that he was, as a vicar, very interested in the development of choral and organ music within a church. In fact, he asked me to look out for somebody who might be interested in being organist at the church. It was at this point in the conversation that my ears pricked up, and I saw an opportunity. To be fair, organists are a rare breed, so it was much easier, therefore, for me to think about offering my services to the church rather than look for anybody else to fulfil the role. Further conversation led me to glean that the church was willing to pay £10 per service which in 1991 was a fair amount.

I cannot remember the month I commenced the appointment, but I think it was around remembrance tide in November. I received a very warm welcome from all the parishioners at

Goodwick church. From the word go I was made to feel one of them, and that warm welcome never left me over the six years I was in post. The Reverend Stephen Thatcher was new to the living, he had only been there a few months himself. We had several meetings and in fact, it was the only church that I've ever had to sign a contract, and it was comprehensive. The musical aspect of activity in the church even had a financial budget, money for the choristers, and I could buy music as and when I chose. This facility was quite rare for a parish church in my locality, because they are usually restrained for financial reasons. I can't remember what the budget was, but I remember it was reasonable for the time.

The choir consisted of young ladies, middle age ladies and gentlemen, and totalled around 16 in number. They thoroughly enjoyed what they did, and each week we would have choir practise on a Sunday afternoon, prior to the evening service at 6:00 pm. The rehearsals were good fun, and everybody looked forward to attending. In fact, being a member of the choir was like being part of a club, and they all loved it. The group brought the best out in me as they were really wonderful people.

 I was still organist at St Mary's church in Whitland at that time, but I was determined that this post would be for me and I would make a success of it. Because the main service at Goodwick church was in the evening each week, meant that I could remain at Whitland church as organist for the morning services. Even that arrangement did not go down all that well with some Whitland parishioners, but quite frankly by now it was just too bad, I was doing this for me. I have very fond memories of my time at St Peters church in Goodwick, of the people there, the members of the choir, and the fun we used to have. In fact, in addition to the singing, the choir enjoyed an annual trip to Oakwood theme park, and they never let me down by misbehaving or any other tomfoolery, they really were a great bunch.

Francesca Didcote and Emma Taylor were two of the senior youth members within the choir, and they took responsibility as team leaders for the day at Oakwood. During the day we rendezvoused a couple of times, met for lunch, and that day Mr Stephens the choirmaster, was 'cool.' It's interesting to note that that's the only church appointment where I was called Mr Stephens, although towards the end I did encourage some of the older youth members as well as the adults to call me Richard. 'Mr Stephens' was far too formal, and I was only 21 years of age after all, and I felt that the salutation of 'Mr 'was still a few years off. I don't think the choristers did had a concept of their choirmaster going on all the rides, but back then I was young and dull enough to do so, and it cemented my relationship with them all. I worked hard at being able to identify with them, because I had always been older than my years, which actually was something I disliked about myself, and I do blame both my personality and church career for this to an extent. It was a philosophy that worked, and we all got on so well, and I was really looked after by everybody during my tenure there.

The first few months at Goodwick was somewhat strange in so much the morning service was officiated by an old gentleman at the organ, who was suffering the onset of dementia (I regret that I have forgotten his name). I met him a few times and bless him, he thought he was in St Pauls Cathedral in London, and we had a conversation about it several times. It's quite sad really that someone of a musical ability can be reduced to this, but it was inevitable that the end was near for him. I will also always be grateful to the late Dennis Gronow, who was head chorister; he sorted everything out on my behalf, which is always a great help, because being Organist and Choirmaster, there is already quite a lot to think about. The choir gentlemen and indeed the juniors were very kind to me from the outset.

As I said earlier, choir practises at Goodwick were before the evening service, between which the ladies of the church, headed by Gina Didcote, provided us with refreshments. There were sandwiches, cakes, biscuits, crisps, and this was the same week after week after week. The family feeling within the church community was second to none, and it was a very vibrant parish with plenty going on to suit everybody.

So, going back to the beginning of how I came to be at St Peter's, the poster, trying to recruit members for my new venture which was the formation of the Haverfordwest Ladies' choir. I always wanted to form my own choir, and I undertook something of a feasibility study to ascertain where the 'gaps in the market' were, and from that I deduced that a ladies' choir was the opening that was very much needed.

For generations, Wales has been dominated by male voice choirs, and whilst this is truly a wonderful heritage, it would be good to offer something of an alternative. The 5[th of]

## Dream, Believe, Achieve

September 1991 was the first rehearsal of the choir, and 18 ladies came along, which was a great result.

From that day on the choir grew in number to 52 at its peak, and over time the standard became such that they established themselves as one of the best female-voice choirs in south Wales. You might be thinking, 'how does he know that?' Quite simply because I have worked with the majority of the ladies' choirs in South Wales over a period of almost 20 years, as you will read about later in the book.

The first chair of the choir was former schoolteacher, Mrs Mabyn Charlton. Mabyn was a lovely lady, very kind of nature and held in high regard by everybody. In fact, she was a little *too* kind and a bit weak as a chair to be honest. I must say at this point that in those days I was a slightly different person to what I am today in so much that I was quite a hard director, and to be fair to the choir, they had a tough time on occasions. I seldom saw eye to eye with the committee, as their decisions were, frankly, ludicrous many a time, but I also knew that to be a democratic society, it was necessary to have a committee. I'm still not overly convinced all these years later that a committee is a good thing. I dare say in some organisations they can be very positive and proactive, but the majority that I have come across are very blinkered in their vision and reticent to try new ideas, and by so doing, they restrict growth of the group. Oh yes, we had many disagreements on a collective basis. As a young and inexperienced conductor, I was not always prepared to compromise. It was my way or the highway, and this wasn't the right philosophy to be honest, but wisdom comes from experience, and at that point I had not had sufficient as far as directing choirs was concerned, and in my defence, I was dealing with considerable stress in my life at that time, and it has many ways of manifesting itself, none of which were particularly pleasant.

During my 4 years with the choir, we performed some wonderful concerts in lovely places, and I remember being part of the annual music festival at Brecon Cathedral in the summer of 1992. This invitation came from my knowing the Organist and Master of the choristers at Brecon, David Gedge, MBE. FRCO., This was the first of a long association with Brecon Cathedral, as I performed there many times since, as an Organist and as a conductor. In fact, I have performed an Organ and piano duet there which was sublime. I also brought my church choir there to sing many services, and it's a delightful cathedral in rural mid Wales.

The first half of the 1990s for me was a difficult time in my life. I was up to my next in course work for my degree, fitting in visits to Reading University (where much of it happened away from home) and studying for examinations. In addition to this by 1993 cracks were starting to appear in my marriage, and this became a living hell. 1991 was also the year I started to teach pupils on a private basis, and my practice grew over 3 years to 40 pupils a week, and two evenings teaching in Haverfordwest (I must point out I still lived in Whitland at this point). My career was hugely successful with 100% pass rate for pupils at examination, but my personal life was a different story. Because all my evenings were taken up with tuition, choirs, committees etc, my studying fell behind slightly in so much that I was one TMA (tutor marked assignment) behind where I should be, and this was causing me major headaches. I would start my open university study about 10pm and carry on right through to about 8am the following morning, and this was quite a regular thing. My day job was at Parc Gwyn crematorium at that time, where I was organist, so it became very difficult juggling everything, and of course I was organist at Goodwick to boot, plus I had problems in my personal life too.

In 1993 it was clear that my marriage was going down the pan. Despite many warnings, in July 1991, I married without truly knowing the person sufficiently well, and I was totally dominated and controlled over every aspect of my life. I lost many pupils because of her unreasonableness towards parents parking at the rear of my property, and she would even cancel them without my knowledge. Even my future father-in-law warned me against marriage, but I was of course, too headstrong to listen, but I paid the price. I often jest that I am the only person I know who was paying for a wedding, honeymoon, student loan and a divorce all at the same time! Thankfully, I was earning good money, but it cost me dear too, and without the help from my dear family I would not have coped. However, in 1994 it became a distant memory as I divorced her for unreasonable behaviour. Thankfully, a few years ago, I had clinical hypnotherapy, and one of the things with this was to erase bad memories of these times, so I cannot tell you too much else, as thankfully I cannot recall all the painful events. One thing I do remember is that I was always accused of not 'paying her enough attention.' In my defence, I was in the final stretches of my degree study, and at that time my assignment and essays were ready for submission (I think I was already a day late sending them), and in her temper she ripped them into shreds, and foolishly I didn't have copies, and they were handwritten!! I didn't see my bed for 48 hours, and by the end of redoing the assignment and a 20,000-word essay, my eyes were almost bleeding! I also recall my prized Bible, which I was presented in 1976 for outstanding contribution as a chorister, had several pages ripped out in anger. It really was a heart-breaking time for me, and possessions like this are irreplaceable and highly sentimental. Some of my certificates were smashed and ripped up during times of temper, and this was a very easy way for her to hurt me deeply. Thank God it's now a very distant memory, and we just were not compatible.

At that time in my life, I was so grateful for the loyal friendship of Doreen Warlow and the late Margaret Burke, who stood by me and watched my back with unwavering loyalty. These two people were priceless, and I will always be grateful for what they did for me, and basically kept me sane at a time everything was crashing down around me. I know full well that I suffered a mental breakdown, as I was studying hard, working hard and had a personal life from hell. My parents were truly wonderful, but they never knew the whole story of how badly I was treated; some things are best kept from parents to prevent them from having sleepless nights. I ought to have told this to my daughter from time to time! Who said that life was meant to be easy?

Committee meetings of the choir would almost always be a quarrel, and often instigated by my ex-wife. I would often have to go into the car park of the Hotel Mariners (where we held our meetings) to console somebody in tears after one of her tirades! I, of course, knew them well, and I had the mental scars to prove it. These public tirades became a regular occurrence, and it was an embarrassment.

Thankfully, in 1994 I could relegate it to the history books forever, never to be thought about again.

In the summer of 1995, the choir undertook a tour of Belgium. The trip had been organised by the then-chair, Ann Sequeira. It all came about after a conversation with Mrs Dr Bowen, who had been organising trips to Belgium with the Jumbulance in the late 1980s. For those of you

who don't know what a Jumbulance is, it is a coach that is fully kitted out as an ambulance inside, complete with medical beds, but it is also like a coach too. They were white and had a blue light on the top!

Anyway, the summer of 1995 was scorching hot, and I remember the departure day very well indeed. I had spent most of the day with Doreen Warlow and her husband Roy, who insisted I have a few 'wee drams' to ensure God speed on the journey. I had a few too many 'wee drams,' and the departure is something of a blur! I do know that we travelled through the night to catch an early morning ferry from Ramsgate to Oostend. Our time in Belgium was fantastic, and the choir performed some exquisite concerts, and I gave organ recitals in Ghent, Oostend and Brugge Cathedrals and at the

English National convent. In fact, the ENC was our accommodation for the week. It was frugal yet comfortable, and breakfast consisted of some stale cheese and bread, strawberry jam, and a croissant. Every morning was the same, and the late Peter Griffiths and Margaret Mills and I had a standing joke about putting the cheese onto the soles of our shoes to re-tread them. Despite the frugal offerings, the mother superior and the sisters were very kind to us, and of course, they are very spiritual and lovely people. The chapel in the convent was breath-taking and very ornate. There was a very fine pipe organ, and it gave me great pleasure to perform an organ recital on it for them.

 The rules in the convent were, as you can imagine, strict. One had to be in by 10pm. Yeah, likely! We hatched a cunning plan. Gail's mum was not one for going onto the town, so she would be in bed by 10pm, or at least back in her room, which overlooked the main street. My 'gang' consisted of me, Peter Daley (the coach driver), Doreen Warlow, Margaret Burke, Margaret's sister from Llawhaden, and of course Gail and Pammy. Peter could do a very convincing impression of an owl hooting, and this was the signal for Margaret to throw the keys down into the street, where we were ready to catch them to let ourselves in. Unless a similar arrangement was in place for others, I'm guessing they must have been all tucked up by 10pm, but I shouldn't think so. It would be 1 or 2am by the time we got in, and the gong to prayer was ringing out at 4am, so sleep was not plentiful, and overnight temperatures didn't drop below 21 degrees, and there was no such thing as air conditioning!! In the daytime, many of us would dangle our legs in the local fountain, it was the only way to cool off.

It was a truly wonderful trip, and for me it was extra special because it was on that trip that Gail and I 'got together' as it were, and we have never looked back. You see, I am convinced that our destiny is mapped for us.

A few weeks prior to the Belgium trip, I was at St Davids Cathedral, playing the organ in a concert. I remember being in the south porch when I gave a young lady a second take. I was certainly bowled over by the loveliness of this individual, and I was introduced to her by her sister, who was a member of my ladies' choir. After a quick chat, it was agreed to meet up after the concert at the Ocean haze hotel in the city.

That was when I met Gail, who has now been my wife for 25 years. Things certainly do move in mysterious ways, and I am convinced that our meeting like that was with the help of a divine intervention. Out of all the people coming into the concert (the Cathedral was full), I happened to be in the porch at that exact moment... I'm glad I was! There is a funny tale to the concert, and yes, it involved me! I was in the organ loft, playing my solo pieces, the screen which conceals the organ console from the nave was retracted so I could be seen. I am not sure why I didn't realise, but I proceeded to pop a huge 'cream line toffee' into my mouth! I juggled with the thing throughout the performance of '*Marche Triomphale*' by Karg Elert, and *Toccata* by Gigout, and I had great difficulty with the copious amount of saliva it produced. It certainly was a great talking point back at the pub afterwards! Gail and I still refer to this now. Her first words to me at the pub were, "I hope you enjoyed that toffee," to which the little group rolled about in laughter. It was funny to be fair, and it is one of those moments that will go down in history.

I've often done little 'stunts' like this, and I have been known to allow a baton to leave my hand on the rostrum at St David's Hall in Cardiff, allowing it to fly through the air and hit the Lord Mayor of Cardiff on the head. It was a very funny moment, and just smile and move on!

By September 1995, it was clear that my time with the ladies' choir had come to an end. My now ex-wife was still attending and making my job extremely difficult by constantly interrupting me and 'correcting' me, and highlighting faults with other singers, and indeed the accompanist. It was wholly embarrassing, and I really was not in a brilliant place, due to the years of stress I had suffered at this point. I worked through a mental breakdown and the only treatment I received was from the help of others and people willing to listen. As a private person this was not easy. One of my more advanced pupils was assistant accompanist of the choir, and she was at the receiving end of one of her many critical outbursts, and so much so that the young lady suffered a severe asthma attack and ended up in hospital. The devil really does exist in people, and I sadly experienced it first-hand.

The accompanist to the choir was Ann Wheeler from Broad Haven. Ann was a retired schoolteacher, and a lovely lady. She wasn't an outstanding accompanist, but she was steady. I have never, in all my conducting years, embarrassed an accompanist when they go wrong. In fact, unless it is detrimental to the choir, I ignore it. The way I see it is that an accompanist will know when they have gone wrong (we all do it) so there is no need to highlight the fact and make them feel foolish. I can honestly say, hand on heart, that not once have I belittled an accompanist, and I am proud of this, because not many conductors can say this. I have always made great strides to be a gentleman in most of my dealings with people as it means a lot to the individual concerned, and as a Christian, I do try to live my life in such a way toward others where I can, but sometimes it can be tough!

As I said, a couple of weeks after the St Davids Cathedral concert, we left for Belgium. Gail was on this trip, and the rest is history! We had a wonderful week, and again, our group of friends were fantastic, and this was certainly one of the best trips I have ever had. My final time with the choir was the AGM of 1995; my appointment had become painful, and it was time to move on. To be fair to the choir there had been times when they were dragged into disputes that they should have been dragged into, and there was no way that my ex-wife would leave, so I had to. I couldn't be in the same room, so there was no alternative. I have always been an orator, so my speech was well planned, and the pitch of it was just right. Throughout my 20 minutes 'address,' you could hear a pin drop, and throughout the whole of it, my ex-wife sat with her head bowed, and there were no interruptions. I walked away that night with my head held high, and with some wonderful

memories, but I felt great sadness because I enjoyed my time
with the choir, and in happier times we had such fun.

I remained Organist and Choirmaster at Goodwick church for
another year after leaving the ladies' choir, but finances
dictated that I could no longer make the trip to Goodwick, and
I didn't have the heart to ask for more money because I knew
that they could not afford it. In addition to this, I was in a
wonderful new relationship, and I wanted time to enjoy it. I
left with a very heavy heart because I had been extremely
happy there. In fact, up to this point, St Peter's Church in
Goodwick was the happiest place I have ever been organist. I
had relinquished my post at St Mary's Whitland in 1994, as
this had naturally exhausted itself, although that too will
always give me heart-warming memories because that is
where my organ career started back in 1980. The people at
Goodwick were very sorry to see me go, but there was no bad
feeling and they wished me well. I still maintain contact with
some of them, especially Gina Didcote and her daughter
Francesca, who is now grown up with a family of her own. It's
sobering when I think that this was 26 years ago! Time waits
for nobody does it? Scary!

This chapter covers the period from 1991 to 1996 as far as
Haverfordwest ladies' choir and Goodwick church are
concerned. Other chapters following will tell you about other
things I did during these years too.

I look back with great pride because I was the only conductor
to have conducted a massed choral gala concert of ladies at Sir

Thomas Picton school in 1992, when we were joined by the choirs of Templeton, Wexford, Glynneath and Neath. Almost 150 singers on stage, and this was the start of a national conducting career that would see me direct choirs up to 800 singers, so look forward to reading all about this in the next chapter '*The national stage.*'

In fact, I conducted several combined choir events at Sir Thomas Picton school hall and made some great friends from the participating choirs. Many of the older singers felt a need to 'mother me,' and one of the members from Glynneath Ladies' Choir invited me to her home on a Saturday near Christmas, and I had the best time, and a feast of food, and the welcome I received was second to none. It gladdens my heart because my conducting and teaching clearly meant a lot to them, and they were gaining such a lot from the experiences. This is what music is all about, enjoyment, making memories and of course central to it all, the opportunity to perform some wonderful music. There is no calling in life better than this, to have a gift that can make such a lasting impression on somebody. I have been very lucky.

When I look at music and the arts now, I hate to see what is happening to them. Lack of funding, lack of empathy and such a promotion of 'core subjects.' To my mind there is nothing to compare with studying the arts as it explores our very being, and it expands our horizons more than anything else, but then I am biased, of course; or put another way, it didn't do me any harm.

I was contacted by the Haverfordwest Ladies' choir back in 2016, when they celebrated their 25th anniversary since I formed them, asking me to be guest of honour at a special concert to mark the occasion. Unfortunately, it clashed with another engagement, and although I perhaps would have felt a little uncomfortable by being there, it was very thoughtful of them to ask me. It just goes to show that there is a deep-seated gratitude for what I did for the choir by getting them together in the first place and sowing the seeds for their future. Sadly, the standard of the choir nowadays is not what it was when I was responsible for them, but there are many factors for this, and the dynamic of membership can be the largest contributor. The most important thing is that they continue to enjoy what they do, and over the past 30 years now this year, it has brought enjoyment to countless individuals, and for this it does warm my heart.

I don't regret my time with the choir at all, and I am very proud that I founded them and that they are still going, as I said, but I do regret the fact that so many of them suffered during a difficult time for me. I am by nature a very private person, and to have one's private life played out in public was horrendous and it drove me to the edge on many an occasion. I do think that if it wasn't for my parents at that time, I would have driven my car off a cliffside somewhere and brought it all to a premature conclusion. Thank God I didn't because I wouldn't have had the chance to write this book!

## CHAPTER 5
### *The National Stage*

It all began in late 1992 when I was asked to be part of a steering group to stage a gala concert for *Save the Children* at the Brangwyn Hall in Swansea, which was going to take place in June 1993. The organiser was Sian James from Abercrave, and she had more passion and drive than anybody I have ever met. She would sell sand to the Arabs without a shadow of a doubt, and her contacts were limitless. The last I knew of Sian she was a labour MP for the Swansea valley, and although I haven't seen her since 1994, I have no doubt that she is a great constituency MP.

I already had associations with WAMF – the welsh amateur music federation in the early 1990s, who were responsible for the management and administration of the National Youth Choir of Wales, which I was involved with. WAMF also had many ladies' choirs as members, so this is where Sian conscripted 250 singers for her gala concert. This was the first concert of its type ever staged in Wales, and it was certainly unchartered waters. The Brangwyn Hall had 2,000 seats, and to make a profit, at least 1,500 of them had to be sold, and this was a huge ask, seeing that ladies' choirs did not have a great following in Wales. I had my doubts that this would work, but Sian was full of optimism, and on the 13th of June 1993 the stage was set.

This was my first time on a national stage as a conductor, and at only 23 years of age it really was a big ask. I was somewhat anxious, but I always try to take everything in my stride, so it was just another engagement, although a *very* prestigious one. The concert followed four massed rehearsals which took place in and around Swansea, and they were very hard work. Massed choir rehearsals are only supposed to facilitate interpretation and 'polish,' but some of the choirs were well behind where they ought to have been, so note-bashing was necessary! Some of the participating choirs' musical directors had doubts that I could pull this off, and some constantly pushed their ideas on me. The host for the evening, as well as one of the soloists, was Beverley Humphreys (BBC). This was the second time I had worked with Beverley, and she is a superb compere and host, and always has the audience 'eating' from the palm of her hand.

The hall was full – 2,000 tickets sold!! It was an outstanding success. The other soloist at the concert was a young harpist from Pen-y-Graig in the Rhondda by the name of Rhian Hanson. She certainly knew her way around a harp, and over the following few years, Rhian and I worked together a couple of times, and we still maintain contact now through social media; she lives with her young family in Northern Ireland, where she has a freelance career, and also appears regularly with the Ulster Symphony Orchestra.

I must pay tribute at this point to my stage manager Colin Rogers. Colin's attention to detail with stage craft was second to none, and there was nobody better to do the job. His military background and fastidious personality meant that would be 100% perfect, and I had no compunction whatsoever in giving him this role. He planned the staging with graph paper, one square representing a singer. He even used coloured pens to shade them in according to their uniform colour.

He was a stickler for perfection and as such would drill the women in the art of walking on and off stage. 'Any old how' would not do for Colin, and they went on and off until he was satisfied. The rehearsals with Colin were always great fun because after a few attempts the women would be getting fed up, and the more they complained, the more he marched them to and fro. They would be expected to all hold their folders the correct way, the left hand, and heaven forbid if one of them was slightly out of sync. He would blow his whistle and dress them down to an inch of their lives and do it again and again until it was perfect. I always let him carry on because I knew the result would be aesthetically pleasing for the audience on the night. Some of the more vocal women from the valleys gave him what they thought, but he didn't care, and he carried on regardless. He was brilliant at what he did, and I always found it amusing. I will tell you more about Colin and his stage antics later.

Following the success of the Brangwyn Hall concert, I found myself rocketed into some sort of musical stardom and held in very high regard by choirs all over the South Wales valleys. It was a great feeling, and whenever I went to valley towns to conduct, such as Tredegar, Newbridge, Caerphilly, Cefn

Hengoed, Ynysybwl, to name but a few, I had the greatest of welcomes, and I could also tell that many of the ladies had their weekly shampoo and set on that day, probably specially for me – I know how to pull 'em!

Following the success of the 1993 Brangwyn Hall concert, I was approached by several choirs who wanted to form an association of ladies' choirs that could further promote the genre and work towards greater recognition. A successful association was already in existence for the male voice choirs, but the ladies' choirs had nothing, although some of them were affiliated to the Welsh Amateur Music federation, but that was not the same thing as a dedicated association.

After calling in some favours, a group of like-minded individuals met in Cardiff, in an office above *oddbins* off-licence, and it was here that the *Welsh association of ladies' choirs* was born in late 1993. I was their first chairman, and the association grew, and almost all the female-voice choirs in south Wales became affiliated.

The Welsh association of Ladies' Choirs, or WALC as we tended to use the acronym, went from strength to strength. At its height we had over 50 choirs affiliated, and about 600 plus members. The association drew a committee together of people with varying expertise, such as an accountant, barrister, teacher of maths, several teachers of music, and local authority councillors, oh, and a funeral director! (you never know…)

In 1994, WALC organised a grand gala concert at the Afan Lido sports centre in Aberavon. Not the most glamorous of venues, but we were aiming to bring together a choir of 600 voices, and the sport hall tier seating area could accommodate just shy of 700 people. The hall itself could accommodate 1,000 seats, so the association booked the necessary people to perform at the gala concert. I was asked to conduct the massed choir and the piano accompanist was Valerie Grenfell, LRAM. ARCM., who was MD of the Grenfell Singers of Swansea and deputy conductor of the Swansea Male choir. I had met Val in 1992 when she performed a joint concert, conducting Swansea male choir and my Haverfordwest Ladies' Choir to mark the 75th anniversary of the Haverfordwest branch of the Royal British Legion. Val was a very able musician, and a competent accompanist. Our guest soloist for the evening was opera singer, soprano Diane Fugue. Diane is a superb singer with a massive technical ability, and she mesmerised the audience with her vocal dexterity. The host and compere for the evening was Alistair Meikle from BBC Wales, who at that time used to be the news anchor on BBC Radio Wales. He was very popular in the 1990s, and he had all the qualities necessary to present the evening. 585 singers took part, and it was an epic concert, with a full capacity hall.

The day before the concert, a friend of mine, Dave Bullock, a lighting engineer, spent many hours putting up lighting rigging and spotlights and follow spots, so that the bog-standard sports hall could look like a half-decent concert venue. I have always been a conductor that likes to be hands on when it comes to organising and helping, and this was no exception. I helped Dave from 6am on the Friday morning until we finished at 11pm that night. All the lighting accessories had to be sought from Cardiff, and I must say that I have never seen so much electrical cable, lighting and connectors in all my life. We had to haul heavy cables up vertical ladders to gantries running adjacent to the roof. There was just enough room to crouch along, at the very apex of the hall. It really was gruelling work for just two people, and I think we both underestimated the job. It was 11pm before we finished, after which we had to drive home to Pembrokeshire. How many conductors would roll their sleeve up and get stuck into this sort of work? I hazard a guess that it would be very few indeed.

On the following day, Saturday, we had to be at the hall by 10am, sorting the stage area, allocating seating, and generally setting up microphones etc. Colin Rogers was once again stage manager, and this time he had a lot more singers to contend with. Colin and Dave Bullock seldom saw eye to eye, and this was from they worked together on concerts in Sir Thomas Picton Hall in Haverfordwest. Two guys that are absolute perfectionists in what they do, but without the ability to compromise. Thankfully, I had known the two of them for many years, and I had a way in which to appease them, and they would do anything for me, but not usually together.

At the Afan Lido, Dave was still adjusting lights when we were ready to start the afternoon stage rehearsal, and the tiers were put into full spotlight and then into darkness. Colin was becoming increasingly annoyed by this, and Dave only had one speed at which he worked, and I think he was going even slower to annoy Colin. After about 30 minutes of going from darkness into light and vice versa, Colin stood on the conductor's rostrum and blew his whistle hard, shouting up to Dave on the gantry to stop what he was doing as he was a bloody nuisance! All hell broke loose, and Dave came down the gantry faster than a chimpanzee, and a somewhat heated altercation took place. Thankfully it was resolved relatively quickly when I politely pointed out that they were not being wholly professional, and that the day was not about their egos. In fact, I could have knocked their heads together on several occasions, and I felt too that they really ought to have had more respect for the event.

The concert was a brilliant success, and this was the start of many that the association organised for their own funds over the next 10 years, all of which I was lucky enough to conduct.

In late 1994 I received a telephone call from an army Major serving in the Royal Regiment of Wales, inviting me to conduct the massed choirs and bands at the 50th anniversary celebration of VJ day the following August. I negotiated a contract, and this was duly signed, which involved me sitting on the steering committee. This was an experience like none other as I was one of only 3 civilians in a room of about 40 people at Cardiff Castle. A typical meeting was chaired by the Colonel, and around the table sat Captains, Majors, Sergeant Majors, Sergeants, and on two occasions even a Brigadier. The army have their own way of doing anything, and I have never heard such straight talking in all my life. 'Bullshit' does not exist around a military table, and whilst it was a breath of fresh air, people were ordered to do things rather than being asked.

## Dream, Believe, Achieve

After the first meeting I requested that Colin Rogers be co-opted onto the steering group, because as a former RSM himself, he could talk their speak, and he would be a suitable interpreter of the 'commands.' It was agreed, and to be fair to Colin he was good, and held his own. Despite being many years retired, he could talk to them at their level, and he knew who to call 'Sir.'

The day in August came, not long after I had returned from conducting and giving organ recitals in Belgium, and the weather was swelteringly hot. In the afternoon of the event was a full-dress rehearsal, and the logistics of this event were so complicated it seemed unreal. In the confines of Cardiff Castle, seating had been erected to accommodate 10,000 people, and the choir stand would accommodate 900 singers. Never had I even begun to think of taking on such an engagement, and the stakes were high. Here was I, 25 years of age, about to conduct Vivaldi's *Gloria* with 850 singers and an orchestra. Vivaldi's *Gloria* was being performed in the first half of the evening, along with some militaria displays, and the second half of the programme was a compilation of repertoire, again interspersed with opera singers and military tattoo. Colin Rogers was the stage marshal for the choirs, and like always, he did a splendid job, and he could deal with the RSM's who were full of their own importance, bellowing and bawling about.

Very unorthodoxly, I had to bring the first movement of the *Gloria* to a halt, exactly as a traffic light system turned from amber to red. In the rehearsal it took a few attempts to get it

right because for me to meet the green light, I had to take the tempi slightly faster than would be usual, but without it misshaping the music in any way, and Vivaldi's opening *'Gloria in Excelsis Deo'* is a fast piece anyway,
without needing to go even faster! I really hoped that most of the singers on stage had used polygrip!!

The reason for the traffic light system was to do with Royal protocol. For the performance the light remained red, and
then turned to amber for the final 1 minute before going to green. When the light turned green, large television screens went live to Buckingham Palace for a message from Her Majesty the Queen, and protocol dictates that the monarch cannot be kept waiting for a second. It was very difficult to achieve because I had to end, with an immediate connection to London. I could not finish ahead of the red light and wait, as the military organisers were quite clear on this. There was certainly a huge amount of pressure on me as conductor, to bring the choirs to a suitable end point.
HRH the Prince of Wales, Prince Charles was in the audience for the concert, along with various other local dignitaries. After the concert I had the opportunity to meet him, and we had a quick chat. I was very impressed by his down to earth nature, and his wit. He winked at me and asked how I managed to keep all the female singers in order, and he said, "I'd rather you than me." It was a great moment.

During the afternoon rehearsal temperatures soared, and I have never in my whole life sweat so much as I did that day. It was over 30 degrees C, and soldiers, dressed in all their finery, including the bear-skin hats, were falling like flies as they were passing out. If I remember correctly, I think a few women from the choir were overcome with the heat also. Initially, Colin was not willing for bottles of water to be brought onto stage, but he had to reneged on this because without water during the performance, the singers would have been in deep trouble.

The evening performance went perfectly, and the soprano, Dame Kiri TeKanawa was outstanding, and what a lovely person she was. The other soloist that evening was Bryn Terfel who enthralled the audience with his deep, well-groomed yet boomy voice. Also, within the soloist pool that evening was Leah-Marian Jones. Leah and I have worked together on a few occasions, and she is a lovely lady with a beautiful soprano voice. It was truly sublime, and the military bands played some solo pieces as well. It was certainly one of those engagements that will never leave the memory, and I am so proud to think that at 25 years of age I managed to carry this off so professionally and with such musicianship. It was a tough ask, and I must admit to feeling out of my depth on times, but you know what... I stood on that rostrum at the start a boy but came off it a man. It certainly was *character forming* shall we say! When one conducts a large, massed choir, your knowledge must be perfect. There are many musical directors who under one baton, sing with their choir, and many of whom are professionally qualified musicians, so everything I do has to be 100% accurate and to bring the best out of the choir. It's not easy conducting several hundred singers, but I enjoyed it, and I have to say I was bloody good at it too.

Just winding back slightly to the autumn of 1994. I was asked to conduct a gala concert at St David's Hall in Cardiff. This was my first occasion appearing there as a conductor, and it was to conduct massed choirs of 500 voices to raise money for Ty Hafan hospice. The presenter for the evening was HTV news anchor (in those days) Nichola Heywood-Thomas.

Rhian Hanson was again on the harp, and the accompanist at the piano was Seimon Morris of Wiston;   Michael Hoeg, the assistant organist of Llandaff Cathedral was at the organ. I knew Michael from previous visits to Llandaff Cathedral, and a finer organist you wouldn't wish to meet. Seimon I had worked together several times as he was a fellow Pembrokeshire musician, and he was the principal accompanist of the Haverfordwest Male Choir in 1991 and I was the deputy accompanist.

This was the first of many occasions that I stood on the conductor's rostrum, and looking back now, they were very proud moments indeed, and in the words of Max Boyce, '*I was that man.*' Max's wife Jean was a long standing member of the Glynneath Ladies' Choir, so I got to know the Boyces quite well.  I met Max on several occasions, and he is such a funny man. I admired him greatly, and he is staunchly proud and passionate of his welsh heritage.

The following year, 1995, I was back at St David's Hall again for the same format concert, this time in aid of Arthritis Care and Wales MIND. Both the concert for Ty Hafan hospice and this one was sell-out events, with 2,000 tickets sold. Every gala concert I conducted at St David's Hall, and I was there every year until 2012, and prior to every concert, I personally attended every participating choir to take them through the programme. I travelled as far as Newport in the East and north to the upper reaches of the Rhondda Valley, to Cwmbran, Treorchy, Ynysybwl and Merthyr, and many other towns in between. As I said earlier, the welcome I received was second to none, but the standard of some of the choirs was upsettingly poor. These choirs were few and far between, but they were enjoying what they did, and that counts for such a lot. The conductors were not vocal teachers, nor were they trained musicians, but they were doing their best. Sadly, many of the choirs had learned some of the concert repertoire incorrectly, and I had to correct many intonational issues and severe timing irregularities. The choirs themselves were always so grateful because I always brought the best out of them, simply because my vibes of confidence rubbed off onto them, and they had a much-needed boost of confidence to really sing out. Whenever I attended a choir rehearsal it was to take their full training session, but I always sat out while they sang one piece. Some of them were great, and others were, well…. at least they enjoyed themselves.

In the years that followed, I conducted every year for charitable causes such as NSPCC, Anthony Nolan Trust, Noah's ark children's hospital of Wales, British heart foundation, Wales MIND. Following the banking crisis of 2008, and the ongoing recession, the concert market started to dry up. Audience numbers were far less, and charities struggled to make a profit, and sponsorship for these large-scale events dried up.

I want to end this chapter by sharing something with you that caused me such hurt, and where I was badly let down by people, I considered friends.

The year was 1998, and the concert at St David's Hall Cardiff, organised by the Welsh association. I was asked to conduct again, and Val Grenfell was piano accompanist for the concert. The second half of the programme was the '*Cavelleria Rusticana*' by Mascagni, with soloist Beverley Humphreys, MBE., but I could not secure an organist. The reason was that all my organ contacts were already booked for that weekend. The cost to get one through an agency was prohibitive, so I offered to play the organ for the second half of the concert, and Val Grenfell to conduct. There was a school of thought circulating at the time that this approach was a little amateurish for a national concert hall, but it was saving such a lot of money, so we went with the plan.
The massed choirs of 500 voices were being joined on the programme by the band of the Royal Regiment of Wales, complete with their mascot, the goat!

Over the years I had got to know the manager of St David's Hall, Yvonne Smith reasonably well, so I arranged organ-practice time with her when the auditorium was free. I went first on my own and had a good couple of hours playing the wonderful grand organ of the hall. The second and final visit, prior to the concert, was with Val Grenfell. I wanted Val to be happy with the registrations of the organ (combination of sounds) and a sort of default volume pre-set. There would have to be minor adjustments on the day itself, due to the absorption by audience and choir, and the volume created by 500 singers. This was built into the planning, and the organ electronic settings were set on my channel and locked into the instrument. This means that when playing, I pressed on a particular thumb or toe piston (the little buttons between the keyboards) then a pre-set array of stops would be withdrawn to create a particular sound and/or volume. Val was happy. One the day itself, as I said, there was need for a slight adjustment, but following a successful rehearsal, everybody was on a high and looking forward to the concert.

It truly was an outstanding gala concert, and the final piece received a standing ovation. It had been hard work but very much worth it, and Val was very pleased with how the second half of the programme had gone, and myself likewise with the first half, which I conducted.

A week after the concert the association held a feedback, or 'wash-up' session at the student's union of Cardiff University. A lot of choirs were represented, and everybody was full of praise for the concert.

Whilst I do value the opinion of others, what I am going to tell you next brought about the ending of my time with the association.

One woman from Crosshands Ladies' Choir said that the organ was too loud and it "spoilt the concert." I am perfectly fine with her comment about the organ being too loud because that was her opinion. I didn't agree with it, however, but she was an untrained ear, so I took the comment with a pinch of salt. I didn't agree that it 'spoilt the concert,' because it simply did not. Val Grenfell, who was by now Chair of the association, nodded her head, and when I questioned her response, she sorts of agreed with the woman. I couldn't believe what I was hearing. She had been full of praise for the organ accompaniment after the concert, and now she had altered her opinion. There was more to this than met the eye, and it was quite simply that they wanted me out. I had been so successful for the association, and now I had outlived my usefulness. In addition to the comments levelled against me, they were utterly ruthless about Colin Rogers, and as he wasn't there to defend himself, I had a problem with that. I spoke out on his behalf and told them in no uncertain terms that he had done a brilliant job and ought to be congratulated instead of being attacked by a load of Piranha. Some of these women were horrid in their tirade against Colin, and it was totally wrong. I closed my folder, and I walked out, never to be associated with them again. It is often strange how 'lay people' can have such opinions that, because of their horrifying nature, can be absorbed by some naïve individuals. It is worth pointing out that on the level 3 bar area of concert venue was Dr Stephen Cleobury, who was organist and director of music at King's College, Cambridge. He was on holiday in Dinas Powys, and had seen the concert advertised, and he came along with friends. I had a quick chat with him, and he was most complimentary, and in fact, he complimented me on my choice of organ registration. So, these sorts of opinions are what matters to me, the people who really do know what they are about, not the idiot who voices some sort of conceited 'opinion,' to be heard, and to temporarily boost their evil ego.

I must point out to you, dear reader, that whilst I am a Christian, and as such, I do forgive people who have wronged me, but I have my limits, and when somebody goes out of their way to wrong me intentionally, I have a long-lasting problem with that, and these people will be eradicated from my consideration forever.

I did conduct 500 massed ladies' voices again at St David's Hall some 10 years later in 2008. Much water had travelled under the bridge over those ten years, but I made it clear from the outset as to what choirs would *not* be allowed to participate, and at no time did the organisers go through the association. This might seem a vindictive thing to do, but I was not ready to forgive the tirade levelled against my friend Colin, nor was I going to smile sweetly in the faces of those who stabbed me in the back so brutally with no justification. No, these choirs were not represented at the concert. I cannot appear false. If I don't like somebody, they know about it. In 51 years, I have never smiled at somebody and it is not truly meant. If I don't like somebody then they have a wide berth, and this was the case in this instance.

The concert in 2018 was in aid of the NSPCC, and in keeping with how I work, I was on the steering committee. After the choirs were on board, the committee received a letter from Val Grenfell from Swansea. None of these people knew who she was, and I stayed dumb! She was writing to ask as to why I had been asked to conduct this concert when the association was in existence, and she was their resident conductor. The old bag was up to her old tricks again, but revenge is a dish best served cold. I didn't mention anything, and the committee agreed not to reply to such a letter.

However, I knew Val's address, and following a meeting at the village hotel in Cardiff, I put it into my trusted sat-nav, and I set off to Morriston. I had not seen or heard from Val since that day in the student's union, but I was determined to seal the deal as it were. When I arrived at her house, she and her husband were hurrying down the garden path, and it was quite obvious to me that they didn't have an appointment, it was all staged, when they saw me pull up outside. She struggled to to get her words out, and I was my usual self, no change of demeanour or tone. I told her that I had been in a meeting about a concert, and I was asking her to consider being the piano accompanist for the concert, because I said that we had worked well together in the past, which was true. This really took the wind from her sails, and she stammered and spluttered, and said that it was 'very kind of me to offer and think of her, and she would think about it and let me know.' Safe to say I never heard from her again. This was a good result after 10 years, and nobody will ever get the better of me again. It may take 10 years to get my own back, but I never forget, and I will always challenge when wronged, and I can challenge harshly too if needed!

Over the years on the national stage, I have worked with some truly wonderful people, such as Beverley Humphreys. MBE., (BBC), Nicola Heywood Thomas (HTV), Sara Edwards (BBC), Alistair Meikle (BBC), Jamie Owen (BBC), Sir Simon Rattle, CBE., Shan Cothi, B.Mus., Sir Bryn Terfel, CBE., Dame Kiri

*Dream, Believe, Achieve*

TeKanawa, DBE., Rebecca Evans, CBE., Wynne Evans, Mark Llewellyn Evans, Diane Fugue, Cecilia Smiga, Leah-Marian Jones, Rhian Hanson, B.Mus., Catrin Finch, OBE., Gwawr Edwards, Terence Gilmore-James, B.Mus. FRCO., Rhiannon Williams, FLCM.LGSM LTCL., Nicola Rose, B.Mus., Huw Tregelles-Williams, OBE., MA FRCO., John Hywel Williams, MBE., Dennis O'Neill, Patricia O'Niell, Dr John Rutter, CBE. D.Mus., Dr Stephen Cleobury, D.Mus FRCO., Dr David Flood, D.Mus. FRCO., Michael Hoeg, B.Mus FRCO., Sir Francis Jackson, CBE.,D.Mus FRCO., Anne Marsden-Thomas, OBE. FRCO., Simon Preston, MA., FRCO., Dr Lionel Dakers, D.Mus.FRCO., and many others on the smaller circuit and somewhat more locally. To be able to share musical work with these greats is very humbling, but it also goes to show how far I had reached in my own musical career, and no amount of money could have paid for these wonderful experiences.

I do not wish this book to be immodest in any way, but this is my chance to recall some wonderful events and opportunities, and when I look at my scrap books, which detail everything I have done, it is like looking at somebody else. My professional life has changed so much as we are now in 2021, and I no longer have the vim or vigour to be as dedicated as I once was. I don't have the drive I once had, and it must be remembered that the 1990s and 2000s were so successful for me, I achieved far more than many people do in a lifetime. Now, in 2021 I don't feel as well as I once did with the various issues with my eyesight, hearing, arthritis, and I don't seem to have the drive and vision anymore to deal with the enormity of such projects, and to manage the stress that comes with them. I never say never, and I am hoping that I have not retired as yet, and that more opportunities will come my way in the coming few years.

The 1994 concert at St David's Hall was also the practical part of my ANCM examination in choral conducting. I had already sat the written part of the examination some weeks earlier. The viva part of the examination, where I was questioned by the examiners about the musical programme was tough, but I passed with flying colours, and was now an Associate of the National College of Music and arts in Choral Conducting. The examiners spent several hours during the rehearsal observing me with the choirs, correcting any intonational problems, and my knowledge of what I was doing. I had a job to do and didn't overly think about the examination but gaining qualifications in choral conducting is something I am extremely proud of. Many, if not all the conductors of local choirs may well be musicians of varying levels of expertise, but to have such qualifications in choral conducting as well as music generally has always placed me at the pinnacle of choral directing. I simply do not wave my arms in the air like some demented praying mantis, but rather my movements direct the choir or orchestra that I am conducting, and my interpretation of the score is transferred skilfully through my baton and my expression. I will always be grateful to the singers because, without their support and cooperation, it would not have been possible. I have always managed to control an extremely responsive choir, and its reality is effortless.

It never ceased to amaze me as to how 'brassy' some of these conductors were from the participating choirs. In everything I have ever done, I am a gentleman, and I wouldn't dream of shouting and bellowing at choirs, or individuals within them. It puts you as conductor on the back foot, and does little for respect from your group, especially female choirs who can be very unforgiving. One can 'get away' with a little more with male choirs, and sometimes they are more difficult to control! I remember one chap from Merthyr Tydfil, who at the time was MD of the Penydarren Ladies' choir. He was a teacher of Mathematics (poor sod was marked for life), and he always would shout and bellow at the choir to be quiet prior to the rehearsals commencing. Don't you just hate that? I used to cringe at the stupidity of the man, shouting and bawling every few minutes, and nobody was taking any notice of him. In fact, they were thinking what a prat he was making of himself. He was clearly a control freak.

When I was ready to start the rehearsal, I would go into the pulpit, raise my arms, and the hush would work its way around the chapel, until I had total silence. Not once did I ever have to shout or any such thing. Thankfully my attitude to these choirs went a long way in their estimation, and I was something of a 'celebrity' in their eyes, and I cannot remember how many souvenir programmes of concerts at St David's Hall I have signed.

When I was autographing these programmes, and receiving such wonderful compliments, it was a hugely proud moment, as I was nothing special, only somebody doing what I had been trained to do, but when I look back, I was facilitating something that meant such a lot to these people, and there is

91

no substitute for that. I must admit to enjoying the adulation, who wouldn't? Yes, I am extremely proud of what I have achieved on the national stage, plus it was an honour. I must say at this stage that not any conductor is allowed to work on the rostrum at St David's Hall. Initially I had to prove my pedigree and references had to be sought. I guess that they had a standard to maintain being the national concert hall of Wales. Thankfully, I didn't detract from that standard, and in fact, I think I did a little bit to enhance it even further. Of course, my time is still ahead to do so much more, and if the opportunities came my way, I would jump at them like a whippet. Sadly, money is now scarce in every walk of life, and large-scale concerts simply do not happen as they once did. To hire these venues is anything upward of £5,000, with larger venues being in the tens of thousands. Without large sums in sponsorship, such concerts cannot get off the ground, and with little guarantee of a full venue. I do hope to grace the rostrum of some prestigious venues again, but for now, I am happy to concentrate on being a straightforward organist in a parish church.

Although the next couple of paragraphs have nothing to do with the 'national stage,' but I didn't know where else to insert this, so do forgive me.

Over many years I have also entertained people within organisations such as nursing and rest homes, as well as day care centres, and entertained at old age pensioner Christmas functions. I started doing this when I was about 11 years of age, and very often I would bring my electric Hammond organ with me, although it was not 'portable' in the true sense of the word, and despite the huge effort that it was, to bring joy to people in the winter of their lives was very important to me. The residents of such places, in the main, used to look forward to me coming, and this too, in its way, made me feel good about myself. I regularly attended Sunnybank home in Narberth, although now the home is no longer there and it is a modern housing estate.

More recently I was under contract with Bush House nursing home in Pembroke. I say, 'more recently,' but I'm going back to about 1994-1997. I would go to the home monthly and play the piano for the residents. The repertoire was mostly old war numbers and classic east-end songs, such as *'My old man said follow the van.'* They were great afternoons and most residents loved it, but one or two who were suffering with dementia, took exception to me being there. Unfortunately, the way that the piano was positioned in the large sitting room, I had my back to the residents who were quietly sitting in chairs, enjoying the music. One or two would come up and smack me on the back with their walking sticks. Sometimes they could really be aggressive, but they were not well and had no concept of what they were doing, bless them. It was £40 an hour, so not to be sneezed at, and worth taking a couple of smacks on the back for! I also negotiated regular visits for the Haverfordwest Ladies' Choir at £100 per time. As I mentioned, I would entertain old-aged pensioners at the Christmas parties, from the start of December, right through until the week before Christmas, and they were delightful events. These wonderful elderly people thoroughly enjoyed it, and I loved seeing their faces light up when I played old songs that they knew well. I would always go round and chat to them all because a minute or so with them meant everything, and many of them were lonely, the only people they saw was at their weekly trip to the day-care centre. They were very happy times in my musical career, and I loved doing it. In fact, I looked forward to doing it. One old lady used to come up to me by means of her zimmer frame, and squeeze a packet of sweets into my hand, or leave them on the organ for me. They were so kind, bless them. I used to entertain the Whitland pensioners when they held their events, either at the restaurant of the milk factory or the common room in St David's Avenue. My grandmother and great aunt and their friends would always be there, so this was a few times a year. My dear grandmother would 'volunteer' my services even without me knowing! I had also brought various choirs there over the years to entertain the residents.

In more recent times I have entertained on a docked cruise ship, and at hotels on New Year's Eve. I once considered a career as a pianist on a cruise liner, but it was but for a fleeting moment. Warpool Court Hotel in St Davids was a recent venue on a New Year's Eve and playing some beautiful ballads on their grand piano were sublime, and couples would be dancing. It was very '*The Ritz*,' but to many people the pianist is invisible, and I'm not overly comfortable with that. Some look at you as if you are far beneath their social standing, and they also ask outlandish requests, and smirk when you politely decline. However, the money is always good, so no good looking a gift horse in the mouth is there? Another regular haunt was the Kensington Mansion at St Bride's. Managed now as timeshare apartments, the large mansion was once a TB hospital. It's location on St Bride's Bay is breath-taking, and the house itself is very stately and grand. I have played the grand piano there several times, and I have also performed there as a vocal soloist, usually performing to an audience of about 50 people, always from across the borders, and very appreciative.

I have also conducted choirs regularly at Kensington Mansion, which is probably better known as St Bride's Castle, although I prefer the former name. Haverfordwest Male Choir were regulars, as was Cantabilé. I've had some wonderful nights there and accompanied several soloists myself too.

I have been so fortunate, as I said earlier, of doing far more than what some people do in a lifetime, and I do sometimes have to pinch myself, especially when I take a trip down memory lane with the help of my many scrap books. It seems to have all happened so long ago, and all too often it is like reading about somebody else, but it was me, and I did it. It kept me on my toes conducting in national venues and with massed choirs, as many of the members were music teachers and proficient musicians, which meant I had to be 100% on top of my game, so it was good for me. People can be so critical, so I always made sure that my directing was perfect from the first upbeat to the final downbeat!

### CHAPTER 6
*Côr Merched De Cymru*

By 1996 I was missing having a resident choir to direct on a weekly basis, and I wanted to form another female-voice choir, but this time with a difference. I wanted to hand-pick members from all over south Wales. Côr Merched De Cymru translated is South Wales Ladies' Choir.

I managed to secure Pencoed comprehensive school's main hall for the weekly rehearsal on a Friday evening, and the musical director of Bridgend Ladies' Choir (Pen y bont), Lesley Walker offered to be the accompanist. Lesley was a school music head, so was proficient, and although she could be a little brusque, we got on well together, and her ability on the ivories was secure.

Every Friday evening myself, Pammy Erickson (my sister-in-law), Doreen Warlow, Margaret Burke and Christine Coaker made the 1½ hour journey to Pencoed for rehearsal. It was a huge commitment, but I had the crem-de-la crem of singers from all over the south wales' corridor and into the valleys. Many of the ladies were already in other choirs, and I did meet some resistance from local choirs, because they knew what standard I could produce, but the formation of this choir was not, in any way, in competition with any existing choir. Barbara Bevan from Newbridge was the first chairlady, and the committee was proactive, and made up of professional people, from schoolteachers to solicitors. I approached the former speaker of the house of commons, Lord Tonypandy, to be the president of the choir and he agreed. Sadly, his health was not good, and he died shortly after accepting the appointment.

In December 1997, the choir performed at Llandaff Cathedral in a Gala concert of music for Christmas, complete with the Llandaff Cathedral Choir and the Llandaff Cathedral school choir, of which, Charlotte Church was a pupil. The headmaster of the cathedral school, Lindsay Gray conducted the school choir, as their head of music, Michael Hoeg, accompanied on the organ. I worked with Lindsay Gray again some years later when he became the principal of the Royal School of Church Music, and I was the Education and Training officer for West Wales area.

This concert was once again part of an examination for me, that of my Fellowship of the Victoria College of Music in Choral Conducting. (FVCM). Fellowship is the highest qualification conferred by a college, and the examination was tough. Dr Tillet from London was the examiner, and he certainly put me through my paces! However, I passed with Honours, a classification only given to 3% of entrants, and I was amongst this number. I couldn't have been prouder. I was also awarded my Fellowship of the Victoria College once again, some years later in pipe organ.

CMDC didn't take on too many engagements, not because we didn't have the opportunities, but because almost every member held membership in another choir, and ladies have many more demands placed upon them than men. My experience with both genres is significant, and it is always easier to get men to commit to an engagement than women, the reason being that there are many factors that are needed to be taken into consideration. Usually women are mothers, homemakers and some tend on their husbands' hand and foot and are dominated. Men just say yes, and that is their commitment, come what may. It really is surprising how many men have control over their wives or partners, it's quite shocking.

The immense travelling to and from Pencoed was taking its toll, and there was a loss of zeal from many people towards the choir. There was no specific reason other than bookings had slowed, and there was not much to prepare for, and we all started to question the need to continue. In reality, local groups and organisations that book choirs for fundraising concerts tended to book their local choir, and there is nothing wrong with this of course. However, it did mean that in turn, Cor Merched De Cymru were not getting the engagements, and after a time of rehearsals only, people lose interest, and I know I certainly did. Despite huge efforts put into the choir, we suffered badly in favour of, as I said, local choirs, but also male voice choirs, because in the South Wales valleys there is a plethora of them, and very good ones too, so a new choir, especially consisting of women was not going to take off in the way I had hoped initially.

Fundraising was something I participated in, and I remember doing an 8-hour organ marathon at the Tabernacle Chapel, the Hayes in Cardiff. Many of the members were outside, complete with their buckets, ready to relive the money-laden shoppers of their cash. My wife Gail is the best people-person I have ever met, and she endears herself naturally to everybody, and that day on the Hayes in Cardiff was no exception. Her bucket alone had £500 in it!! The collection on the street raised something in the region of £2,500, which was an excellent result. At the end of the gruelling 8-hour playing of the organ, with only 5 minutes every hour to make nature's call, there was a couple of hours grace before I was conducting the choir in a concert at the same venue.

We were joined that evening by the wonderful Maesteg Children's choir, who I had worked with in St David's Hall the year before, and I was also their vice-president. The Maesteg Children's choir were an institution, founded by their conductor, Enid Sian Hughes, LWCMD FETC., and her mum, Beatrice Alsop-Jones, ALCM., I got to know Sian and Beatrice well, and I enjoyed several visits to the local school in Maesteg on a Saturday morning to give the kids some encouragement, and to conduct them in readiness for joining 500 ladies in concert at St David's Hall. They joined in for a performance of Adolphe Adam's '*O Holy night*,' and Sian was the soloist. It was truly breath-taking, and I have to say that these kids were brilliant. Gail and I were VIP guests for many years at their annual concert at Maesteg Town Hall, which was always a sell-out gig, and well worth the journey from Pembrokeshire. For many years, Sian's mum Beatrice was the accompanist, and she was a very fine pianist. Sadly, in recent years she suffered a severe stroke, which meant her piano playing days were over. Following Beatrice's tenture as accompanist, Ryan Wood,

FETC., became their accompanist, and a well-established accompanist he is in those areas. I remember visiting Beatrice in the Princess of Wales hospital in Bridgend, and it was not the Beatrice I knew, but thankfully that was about 10 years ago, and she has made a good recovery, and now resides in a nursing home.

Côr Merched De Cymru closed its doors as it were, only a few years after formation, and I didn't miss it from the travelling point of view, but I did miss the members, many of whom were much fun. The thing worth noting, the women from the Rhondda Valleys are tough to the core, but every so witty, and they are genuine, salt of the earth people, with no airs or graces. I had incredible fun as they would deliver their one-liners, and some of them had to be handled with kid gloves, because they would bite if pushed too hard! They were great times, and like all great things, there must be an end. I didn't achieve everything that I set out to achieve with the CMDC, but nevertheless it was great when it lasted, and I met some lovely people, and I will never forget their kindness to me. It was sad that such a good choir had to come to an end, but I guess the south wales area was saturated by ladies' choirs in many of the towns, and when concert opportunities came up, it went to the well-established choirs. It was worth a try of course.

I was always impressed by their passion and will to do well, and this applies to all ladies' choirs in Wales that I worked with. The effort they put into their music making was always 100%, and as a conductor, nothing more can be requested from a singer. The effort put into something is sometimes worth more than the attainment.

Time passes so quickly, and one successful concert I recall directing with the CMDC was for the 75th anniversary of the Haverfordwest branch of the Royal British Legion, and this year (2021), they celebrate their 100th anniversary. I can recall this concert as if it happened yesterday, and to realise how quickly 25 years has passed is frightening.

One element I did find difficult to cope with, generally with ladies' choirs, was the fussing that seemed to manifest itself in many of the members. I detest intensely arriving at a rehearsal venue and people pestering you before you settle in. I hate it with a passion. I like to arrive, set up, say hello to everybody 'remotely' as I call it, and then I can speak to people. Women in choirs can fuss for Britain, and it used to drive me round the bend. My personality is such that I don't take on board fussing and fuss pots as they drive me to distraction. All too often what they are fussing about is of no real significance, nor is it worthy of wasting vast amounts of breath discussing it. It was always a fine balance to get right because I never wanted to appear rude or off-hand to any of these members, because to them, I guess, their fussing served some sort of purpose. I listened quickly to them, and then dispelled it rather swiftly. Over the years it became one of my strengths, and I could shut somebody up in seconds, and still they thought I had taken on board everything they had fussed about. The truth is that I had no clue as to what they were squawking on about, as most of it was timewasting, and many people, believe it or not, 'like' to be seen talking to the conductor. Despite what you may think, members of the male voice choir could be as bad, and no sooner than I would turn up, there would be somebody bombarding me with information, and I really detest this. I like to settle in, as I say, and then breathe a little. I am very exacting as to how I conduct myself and others have to interact with me, and it's not me being difficult at all, but it is me being me.

## Chapter 7
*The Royal School of Church Music*

My association with the Royal School of Church Music (RSCM) first came about in 1994, when I was asked to join the west wales area committee. The then-chairman was Lt. Col.David Smith, who was my predecessor at St Martin's Church in Haverfordwest, and a former asst organist at Rochester Cathedral.

For the uninitiated, the Royal School of Church Music is a learned body, teaching college for all things church music. It administers the very successful chorister award scheme, *voice for life,* the Dean's award, Bishop's award, and the St Cecelia award for choristers. Incidentally, I achieved all three back in the day of starched ruffs! It also trains organists in the art of hymn accompaniment and chants. It really is *everything* in the field of church music.

It has several local area committees across the United Kingdom and indeed many other countries, all responsible for the promotion of church music in all its forms. Predominately an Anglican institution, but in recent decades it has become interdenominational, simply because the music trends in places of worship is changing, and many more styles and cultures are part of the bigger picture.

When I first got involved, the west wales area committee were stagnant, and events were very few and far between. The area secretary at that time was Ian Jones, LLB.,JP., who later became one of my bass choristers at St Mary's in Pembroke. Ian was one of life's great administrators and a perfectionist in the extreme, but I think the whole committee lacked a vision for the future, and churches then tended to be very insular and not open to ideas either.

It was very difficult to motivate people to explore new ideas or to venture out of their comfort zone. For me, joining the committee, I could not simply attend and twiddle my thumbs. I was sitting there and witnessing a scene from *The Vicar of Dibley,* with the discussions going round in circles, and digression like it was going out of fashion. I found it somewhat infuriating to be honest, and a total waste of my time.

I could not give a vast commitment in the beginning simply because I was coming the latter stages of my OU degree, but I did what I could. I am, by nature, a very determined and single-minded person. I have enthusiasm for a project by the bucket full, and perhaps too much so because I become easily dispirited when others do not share the same vim and vigour for a project as I do. However, this aside, it was going nowhere, and there was little guidance from 'central office,' which was Addington Palace in Croydon. The communication between HQ and the areas greatly improved with the appointment of regional commissioners, and this was a strategic link to the area secretaries. I think it fair to say that the RSCM became somewhat stale and lost its way somewhat.

The RSCM at Addington Palace ran some very successful residential courses for organists and choir directors, as well as some very informative publications and resources for choristers, such as the much-coveted red, royal blue and light blue medals and ribbons of the chorister training scheme (later to become *voice for life*).

I attended a couple of courses at the RSCM, facilitated by international concert organist and teacher, Ann Marsden-Thomas, MBE, FRSCM, ARAM, FRCO, BMus, Dip RAM, ARCM, LRAM.,

Ann was also Organist and Director of Music at St Giles' Church, Cripplegate in London, one of the very few female directors at that time, and indeed now. In fact, Ann founded the international women's organist association in 2019, with a launch event at the Royal Festival Hall. She currently teaches at the Royal academy of Music, where she teaches the LRAM course. I have attended some of her masterclasses in years past, and they are brilliant, and she is very much an authority on the music of J.S. Bach.

All courses and training have always been friendly and aimed at encouraging the amateur musician to become a better church organist, and the courses are wonderfully tailored to suit their needs, and they are never too deep or beyond the comprehension of the students attending.

In more recent years I directed one such course, and it taught me never to judge people, certainly by their appearance or outward demeanour. In my group was about 20 delegates, all with varying participations in church music. Some were choristers, some were organists, some were what we knew as 'reluctant' organists, and there were others who were simply

105

'just interested.' As I may have said earlier, church music brings with it a degree of snobbery, of high ideas and opinions. There was one delegate on the course who, by appearance, one would cross the street to avoid. He had a pink Mohican hairstyle (they were in vogue in those days), pins through his nose and mouth, and had a denim jacket with holes in, and it was embellished with badges. He stood out like a sore thumb, and the more conventional in the group didn't mix with him. He spoke very well and was clearly a well-read type. At the end of the course, he was the only one who came and shook me by the hand and thanked me for a wonderfully interesting course, which enthused him greatly. It transpired that he had a Doctorate in Physics from Cambridge, yet by appearance he looked as if his home was under the flyover in Camden. How wrong we can be about individuals, and this incident has remained in my mind ever since. It wasn't the snobs in their Sunday best who were the Christians that day, but rather the one who looked like a thug, but was far from it. It just goes to illustrate the adage, *'never judge a book by the cover.'*

When Lt. Col. David Smith retired as Chairman of the west wales committee, it was at that point the RSCM decided that the chairman of the committee would be the resident organist and master of the choristers at St Davids Cathedral. This was, in my opinion, rather a virtuous move because after all, the cathedral director of music is a professional in the field, so would be an ideal candidate to lead the way. I was sadly wrong in my philosophy. The first cathedral organist chair was Geraint Bowen, and he was far less than useless! A lovely chap in himself but as aloof as the fairies that fly out of the garden hedge at night. He had little or no interest in the RSCM, and he took the role on under duress. His appointment didn't really make any difference to us as an area committee, we saw no improvement in any of our activities, and we didn't see any more events being arranged. The area committee tended to arrange reluctant organist days which were aimed at basically a mediocre piano player who wanted to aspire to the pipe organ. At these events we had some useful participants, but the majority ought to have stayed at home, and it was a simple waste of time and of everybody's energy. There was a lady from Haverfordwest who attended all the reluctant organist days, and in later years when Simon Pearce and I would be responsible for taking the courses, we used to try hard not to pee our pants through laughter, we had to always remain professional, but it was extremely difficult. The lady in question thought that she was playing some sort of theatre organ, a Hammond instrument or even better a Wurlitzer, because she used the swell expression pedal as if she was on a harmonium! The organ crescendo and diminuendo faster than a Viper on speed, and it was hilarious, bless her.

The important thing in all these events that the Royal school of church music arranged was the fact that they were to be enjoyed by the delegates, and of course if this was achieved then our aim two had been met. Geraint Bowen did not remain at St Davids terribly long, as he took up an equivalent post at Hereford Cathedral. He was replaced by Timothy Noon, MA (Oxon), B.Mus (Oxon) FRCO FRSCM FRSA., who was fresh from Canterbury Cathedral where he had been assistant organist. Tim Noon was young, in his middle to late twenties, and a brilliant musician. He had studied at Christ College, Oxford and was a prize-winning fellow of the Royal College of Organists and a Fellow of the Royal School of Church Music. Tim was a breath of fresh air, and he took command of everything 'RSCM' within the Diocese.

Ian Jones had now left the committee, and I was appointed area Secretary in his place. Tim and I worked well together as officers of the RSCM. The treasurer was Paul Watkins, who was, at that time, Choirmaster at St Peter's in Carmarthen, but I could never work out as to why he took on the role because he was less than useless at it. Invoices often remained unpaid, and he was a nightmare to pay anything. As the area secretary I was receiving 'phone calls from various places saying that we still owed them money. Eventually the committee, and Tim had certainly had enough of this nonsense, and he resigned from the RSCM. Of course, like many of these sorts, it was everybody else's fault. Paul and I got on well personally, and I helped him out in his choirs many times when they sang services at Cathedrals during the choir recesses in the summer.

I cannot remember how long it was before I was appointed the Education and Training officer for the west wales area. This was an important role because I was responsible for the management of the chorister training scheme, *voice for life,* and for making the necessary arrangements for the choristers to sit their examination. During my time as ETO, most entrants for the Dean's and Bishop's awards were members of the cathedral choir, but we did have a small number from other churches too. David Leeke, the Organist and Master of

the Choristers at Shewsbury abbey, and later St Chad's
Shrewsbury was the appointed examiner, and we had many a
happy Saturday spent examining in the Cathedral. David and
I became friends, and over the years which followed I played
the organ at St Chad's, and the male voice choir and Cantabilé
gave concerts there as part of their *'music in the round'* season.
In all, I spent 15 years as part of the RSCM and 13 years
working as Education and training officer. Part of my role was
also to organise the annual festival service at St Davids
Cathedral, which always took place on a Saturday in May. The
amalgamated choir, made up of affiliated choirs, would
rehearse in the afternoon, and then around 5pm there would
be a festival service, usually directed by Timothy Noon, but
one year we invited Dr David Flood, the Organist and Director
of Music at Canterbury Cathedral. It was truly a wonderful
day, and everybody was reinvigorated to carry on developing
the music within their own parishes. Part of the ETO role was
as a music development officer, and I worked on this in
conjunction with the Revd Jonathan Copus, MA LGSM., himself
a composer and a fine musician, who used to work for the BBC
producing Songs of Praise, and teaching music in a secondary
school. Jonathan and I developed the programme from
scratch, which was comprehensive, aimed at developing music
within churches, and encouraging the development of choirs.
We would do the marketing and recruitment work on behalf
of the affiliated church, and we would also go along to train
the organist and indeed the choir themselves. The RSCM had
considerable uptake of this course, so much so that Jonathan
and I were going all over the three counties with it, and we also

had to bring in Tim Noon as a third person as there were so many churches wanting to take advantage of this new scheme.

It is strange though as to how much apathy is out there within these churches for the development of their music. All too often they allow the negativity to control their thinking, and that was even before we had attempted anything. I had heard the excuse several times, 'oh, we tried that, it doesn't work here.' It used to annoy me somewhat because these were lay people who didn't have the necessary expertise to bring the development to fruition, and they were the ones asking for help! It was quite strange to understand where they were coming from on times. I am never left baffled as to why so many churches are emptying faster than water from a bucket full of holes, these people are not making their services attractive, they are not encouraging new growth, they are loathed to any change, and they are not open to new ideas. I used to get quite stern with some members of the clergy who always thought they knew best when clearly, they didn't. I did say to one such cleric, "you are qualified I presume to preach the word of God from the pulpit are you not, and I am qualified to develop your musical programme, so I do suggest that we stick to our relevant specialties and throw your cap of negativity in the bin!" They were words wisely spoken because after that we didn't have any resistance, and their music developed successfully.

Congregations too are often full of negativity and not willing to embrace new ideas, and I despair as to how this attitude is going to facilitate growth for the future; sadly, it is not. Old fuddy-duddies that don't want to see youth in the churches, and who hog seats on church committees for decades, preventing any newcomers from gaining entry to the inner sanctum. I admire commitment of these stalwarts, and they are often the backbone of churches, by the service that they have given, but it is very important to know when our sell-by date is up. It is vital to know when to step aside or down, and to allow younger people to take over, and carry on the torch so to speak, into the future. It cannot be *how it shall be, forever and ever, Amen.* We **must** allow new growth, we **must** embrace new ideas, and we **must,** from time to time, step outside our comfort zones. When we do, we are surprised to find there is often far better on the horizons. I really do admire, however, the older generation who keep our places of worship going, and all too often they stay on in roles *because* there is no new blood, and to stand down would make them feel as if they are letting their congregations down, and of course, they secretly enjoy what they do. Very often it gives a purpose to the winter of their lives, and I guess it is all about finding the right balance.

There is no easy answer, and when I was part of the RSCM's development team, it was discussed at length by
many experts. The development of music in churches today is fraught with difficulties, mostly because we live in an ever-increasing secular society.
For the past 15 years or so, church choirs have been steadily on the decline. It is difficult, if not impossible, to attract teenagers from scratch, and Sunday is no longer a day of rest or a go-to-church or chapel day. I wholeheartedly disagreed

with sports clubs and the like undertaking training on a Sunday; Saturday should have been sufficient. Another nail in the coffin of sacred Sunday was the introduction of Sunday trading laws. I must also stretch my neck out somewhat further when I say that another reason why it is so difficult to recruit young people into a church choir is that for them, services are often stiff and stuffy, and they have difficulty identifying with what is going on. Choirs that manage to recruit several young people are often successful and continue to grow, because they see going to choir as being part of a club, a mutual interest.

I remember some years ago when a very musical young man became a lay clerk in the Cathedral choir, but in fact was an atheist. Was this right and proper? He had no belief, yet he could robe and sing sacred music each time he entered the building. I failed to understand as to how somebody could balance these two extremes from each other, but it must have been beneficial to a career or pathway he was choosing, or to look good on a CV. I have my difficulties with this to be honest.

Two very big successes of my time with the RSCM West Wales, was bringing the international composer and choral director, Dr John Rutter to Pembrokeshire. Dr Rutter, or simply John Rutter as he likes to be known, was a delightful man to talk to, and he guided me through the process of organising two of his choral singing days. They took place in the Sir Thomas Picton school hall in Haverfordwest, and the first one attracted more than 600 singers. At £10 a ticket, it raised considerable revenue for the area funds. Singers came from far and wide to the singing day. People came from Ireland, York, and parts of Devon; such was the appeal of John Rutter and his music.

My wife and I met up with John Rutter the night before at the Hotel Mariners in Haverfordwest, and we enjoyed a few whiskies together.

He certainly liked his fire water! What struck me about John was his intense passion for what he did. His enthusiasm was very infectious, and he oozed genius. He was, for some years, Director, and Professor of Music at Clare College, Cambridge University, and he remains director of the professional choir, The Cambridge Singers. John chose the musical programme he wanted, and of course it was a great opportunity for him to promote new anthologies and octavo pieces. If you think about it, we had to ensure that 600 copies of each book and piece he required. When he supplied me with the list, I contacted a very helpful young lady in the lending library at Oxford University Press. She confirmed that everything was available, and it was being delivered to my home address, 3 days prior to the event. Almost 2 tonnes of music were delivered on three pallets! I have never seen so much music at any one time, all of which had to be handballed into my home. Gail and lifted boxes for hours, well into the evening, and they filled our living room, hallway, inner hallway, and our bedroom. 600 copies of everything!! I was very grateful to Tom Pearce of St Mary's Pembroke, Ian and Sue Jones who helped to take the music to the school on the day of the event. Placing 600 copies of everything onto the seats was also a mammoth task. All of the music used that day was available for sale at the end of the event, and many hundreds of copies were sold. The RSCM received a percentage of the sales. John Rutter brought copies of his CDs for sale, from his own company *Collegium records,* and several hundred were sold. These events were certainly a win-win situation for all concerned.

As I said, we held two of these events, some two years apart, raising well over £12,000 for the area funds. These events were hugely successful, and not only did it bring one of the foremost composers to Pembrokeshire, it introduced 1,200 singers to new music, or certainly to his wonderful music.

I left the RSCM at the same time as Timothy Noon. I had achieved much, and whilst on the face of it, it looked that we were 'deserting' the area, there was plenty of expertise remaining on the committee, and after so many years, it was time to allow new buds to flourish. I also couldn't imagine working alongside another chair who would be as good as Tim, so I jumped from the raft before it all become boring. I loved my time associated with the RSCM, and I look back on my time there with much pleasure.

Over the years I have had the pleasure of accompanying much of Rutter's music, and one such occasion was his *Requiem* at the Symphony Hall in Birmingham, and closer
to home at St Martin's Church, Laugharne.   I have also accompanied several flautists with his '*Suite Antique*,' written for piano and flute, as well as '*With the spirit,'* a song cycle, with his arrangement of negro spirituals, many of which are maliciously difficult, and not really my cup of tea to be honest.

As I said, I thoroughly enjoyed my time with the RSCM, and I am proud of the work I did to help the cause. I look back and hope that from the little acorns I planted in many parts of the diocese did eventually turn into oaks. There was a good team in West Wales, and I was extremely proud to be part of it. In 2009 I was presented with an award of special service in recognition of my work with the RSCM in West Wales. This was presented to me on behalf of the principal, Lindsay Gray, and the executive council, and presented at St David's Cathedral.

Looking back, I think the highlight of my time with the RSCM was meeting people who were interested in 'having a go,' and wanting to experience more of the organ. Many of them were not very good, and they were never going to 'make the grade' as it were, but their enthusiasm was infectious. The youngster's reaction when an Open Metal 32' stop was played on the pedal, which made their teeth rattle! If, during these 15 years, I managed to bring one person into church music, then I will have done my job.

As I mentioned earlier, Ann Marsden-Thomas is one of the great movers and shakers in the world of organ playing, and for generations, church and cathedral music has been hugely dominated by men. Up until a few years ago, there wasn't a female Director of Music or Organist in any of our UK Cathedrals. Now we have several, and this must be a good thing. I think tradition all centred around choirs consisting of men and boys. Don't get me wrong, girls cannot, no matter how good they are, replicate the pure hoot of a good treble (I was one, so I know lol!) I personally, don't think mixing of the genres in a Cathedral choir is a good thing, but fully advocate a separate girls' choir to coexist with the traditional choir of men and boys. Cathedral music and indeed closer to home, our own church music is very much under threat. It is under threat from that cancer called secularism, and lack of resources, i.e., money. The covid pandemic has cost our great places of worship many hundreds of thousands of pounds, and for some, there was no recovery, and sadly the first resource to be scrapped is always the music department. I don't want to get my soap box out again, but if such places want to save amounts of cash, get rid of the copious amount of clergy hanging about in these places. Cathedrals don't need the hangers-on. A Dean and Sub-Dean is sufficient. There ought to be a director of music, deputy, organ scholar and a PA for the music department and that is it. Far too much money is being absorbed with unessential services, unessential office staff and even 'managers' in our places of worship. Get rid of them, and concentrate on a good, solid nucleus to bring glory to God in the best way possible, and Music has been part of this praise and worship for thousands of years. I really do worry for the future of our Cathedral's musical tradition, and indeed churches too, with the advent of CD players, guitars and projector screens. 'Funky news for modern man,' is being allowed to creep in, to make us more 'appealing' to today's society. What crap! Some things must be kept in their traditional form. History is important and must be maintained, not diluted to suite the namby-pamby ways of this country. If Churches and Cathedrals cease to be places of great musical tradition, then there will be a greatly reduced need to study the organ, and this too will dry up. We are fast losing a cultured nation, so I really do fear for the future of our wonderful places of worship and their music. Of course, it costs a considerable amount of money to run a successful choir in a Cathedral, but a lot of the money is derived from wealthy parents who can afford to send their child to the choir school, with its, for many, prohibitive fees, yet the organist, in comparison, receives a pittance. Who is benefitting? It's a very deep topic for greater minds than I to work out, but I don't think the next 40 years will be as good as the last. One observation I will point out to you is that all too often it is seen as an 'elitist' activity, and sadly it rather is. Cathedral choristers are almost always derived from wealthy homes, where parents can afford the fees payable (scholarships don't cover the whole amount). The youngsters are usually so bright and musical that they sound like somebody in their fifties, and it really is a case of 'birds of a feather…'and all that.

There has always been much debate about the rich verses the poor, and the opportunities one can get with the former. It really is so wrong, as I have known some brilliant trebles try to get into choir schools from very poor and deprived backgrounds, but they simply don't fit in to this very specialised, privileged, stiff, and snobby environment; very sad. At the end of term at choir school, usually after the Christmas morning service, or perhaps midnight mass if you are lucky, the parents all pull up in their Bentleys and Jaguars, Mercedes and all these sorts of cars, with twangs that would put the Queen to shame. It is a world slightly removed from the reality of everyday life in so many ways. It is for some people, but for me boarding school can be detrimental; it very much depends on the ability of the child to cope with the often-draconian approach and regimented routine, yet some youngsters thrive on it, and good for them if they do I say. There is a huge differential between Cathedral choirs, their schools, and local church choirs, not only in the standard and indeed the tuition, but in the ethos. It is very old-fashioned, and all the choristers are the most well-behaved kids in Christendom and are very bright musically and academically too. They are looked after by a matron who is in-charge of the dormitories within the choir school accommodation. It really is a very old-fashioned, discipline and manners-rich environment, far removed from the modern world, an ethos that has not evolved too much since the time of John Blow and Maurice Greene. Having said all of this, the contribution these institutions make to our choral heritage is priceless, and a Cathedral without a choir would be a very sad and lifeless institution, full of boring regularity and fastidiousness.

## Chapter 8
*Can you do me a favour?*

When you are a musician, you are always everybody's best friend when they need a favour. Being a musician, particularly an organist, you are always in demand for this or that service, especially singing festivals and Cymanfa Ganu. In fact, your services are needed in many places.

I have lost count over the years how many requests I have received to help here and there, but often on a gratis basis. My dear mother-in-law once said to me, "the jugs on the sideboard are full of 'thank yous.'" Dr Michael Smith once said, "know your worth and charge accordingly." Wise words, but not that practical in Pembrokeshire I hasten to add. In fact, my friend Timothy Noon, who is now Organist and Master of the Choristers and Director of Music at Exeter Cathedral, told me on many occasions that my fees were ludicrously low.

Prof William Mathias, the welsh composer, who was brought up in my hometown, told me in 1998 before a concert I was performing at and he was the president of, that Wales is dominated by amateur musicians who people don't pay for, and when it comes to paying for a professional, the edges of reason bleed into obscurity. This is true, because many musicians in Pembrokeshire do it purely for pleasure, and as such, this is an amateur pastime, and many of this group do not charge for their services. When one does charge for services, you can expect to hear every excuse known to man, because everybody wants, or should I say, expects a freebie.

I was once contacted by a curate from St John's Church in Pembroke Dock, who was enquiring if I could play for a wedding at the church. The reason I was approached was because the couple wanted *Toccata* from Widor's 5th symphony as the recessional voluntary, and the resident organist at St John's at that time, could not play it. This didn't surprise me as the piece is fiendish, and it does call for an organist to play it rather than a piano-playing 'organist' (if you know what I mean). My fee then was £75.00, and when I informed her of this, the tone of the conversation altered slightly, and she promised to "come back to me," those famous words, which meant that I was never to hear from her again. They would have been more than happy for me to have played for no remuneration. I know God loves a 'cheerful giver,' but there are limits!

It never ceases to amaze me how much money is splashed out on the modern-day wedding. Literally hundreds of pounds on fripperies, yet when it comes to paying a church fee and an organist, it is almost a 'suck through the teeth moment,' and many of these couples will never be seen of again once the big day is over.

I have to say at this point that Revd Dr Harri Williams, my former vicar at St Katharine's Church *always* endorsed my fees, and I *always* had the money upfront. There was never a discussion, and he always made it perfectly clear that the organist at St Katharine's was a professionally qualified musician, and as such there was a professional fee to be paid. His support was always very much appreciated. Harri was a good support, and being a musician himself, he understood how it needed to work.

I have helped fellow colleagues' numerous times by singing bass in the choirs of St Paul's Church in Sketty, Swansea, and at St Mary's in Tenby, and St Mary's Church in Fishguard. The former was an annual event, joining the choir to boost their gentlemen on occasions when we sang at Cathedrals during the summer breaks. The latter was annually for the Tenby Arts Festival. I have also sung in the choir of St Mary's Church, Fishguard, for a song of praise.

In fact, I have conducted the congregational singing at St Mary's Fishguard for a song of praise, and I have also conducted an RSCM event there, a scratch performance of Stainer's *Crucifixion.* I have only ever charged to play at weddings as an organist and helping these various church choirs has always been as a favour to the resident organist or incumbent. Despite not earning money from it, it is good to help people out from time to time, and when one is asked, it means that one is highly thought of I suppose.

Christmas time is always a busy time for an organist, and up until 2019, It would be nothing to play for 10 or so carol services throughout the month of December. The traditional crib service and the carol service of the Brownies and Guides in Haverfordwest was an experience. The noise these kids would make was unbelievable, therefore playing the organ preservice was absolutely a non-starter! I also accompanied Tasker-Milward Comprehensive school's Christmas Carol service some years at St Mary's Church in Haverfordwest.

Each year, the school 'orchestra' would accompany some of the carols *with* the organ, and the tempo was so slow; I am not sure what their head of music was thinking of! When I accompanied them for a second time, I suggested that the organ accompany most of the carols on its own, and she agreed. The orchestra did a few, which gave me some breathing space! I also worked quite closely with the music teacher in Barn Street CP school, and I worked with the children on many little concerts and performances that they gave. I was a school governor at that time, and it gave me much pleasure to attend the school and accompany their singing and giving little tips here and there. The teaching staff were very grateful, and I developed a good working relationship with them all.

I would also receive a request from Revd Geoffrey Gwyther or Revd Geoffrey Eynon, chaplains at Withybush General Hospital, to play the organ at St Luke's chapel for the annual service of nine lessons and carols in the early part of December. This too is a little bit of an 'experience,' simply because of the size of the chapel. It is but a small room with no acoustical properties, and it is usually very hot in there. The organisers try to squeeze patients in beds into the room, and it is all a little hotch potch to be honest. Over recent years I have been so booked up in December that I have not been able to accept the invitation.

What I have also experienced over the years is that people love you when you keep saying 'yes,' but the moment you say 'no,' it all changes. You are no longer 'useful' to them, and it's unlikely that you are asked again. I have experienced this many times, and it has led me to believe that people are not loyal to you, but rather loyal to their **need** of you. It goes to prove that these organisers don't care *who* is playing as long as there *is* a player. It is a sad, but nevertheless a true reflection of human nature today, and more surprisingly, many of these people call themselves Christians. Of course, in the great scheme of things the only thing that matters is that these events have somebody to play the organ, but to me, a one-off time of unavailability does not mean I am unavailable forever more.

I have also accompanied many instrumentalists on piano at concerts across the county, and one such musician I have accompanied on numerous occasions is Miss Alex Lucas, MA, B.Mus. (Hons) Dip ABRSM., Alex was, for many years, a pupil of mine before going off to study music, and she is now a professional in her own right. I also accompanied her in the Edwin Braun Halle in Oberkirch, Germany. My preference is always to accompany vocalists, and I have accompanied the following local singers on several occasions: Joy Cornock, B.Mus. Dip ABRSM., Lowri Flur Davies, Trystan Llyr Griffiths, Pippa Bevan, Hilary Riley, B.Mus., and Mirelle Ryan. Hilary and Mirelle were vocal students of mine, Hilary studied for her LRSM examination in recent years, and Mirelle gained her Grade 6 examination during her time with me, and another vocal student Emma Griffiths who gained her grade 6.

I have also accompanied on organ further afield, although these were professionally funded engagements. I played for a gala concert of combined male voice choirs at Cheltenham Town Hall for a welsh society concert, under the baton of Dr Terry James, to celebrate St David's day. I have also accompanied at St Giles' Church in Wrexham, a performance of Haydn's *Stabat Mater.* I have also accompanied the local mixed choir, Landsker Singers many times in performances of Handel's *Messiah,* and accompanied them at a concert in Minehead, Somerset. By my own admission, I am not 'inherently' an accompanist, as I think they are a special breed of individuals, and it really is a specialised skill. I feel a huge burden of responsibility being an accompanist, whereas if you are a soloist, then a mistake is at your own peril, without risking the welfare of the performance of somebody else. I have, of course, accompanied many performers, and I very seldom refuse, but if I had to choose something I enjoyed least of all, accompanying would probably be it.

One 'help-out' that I thoroughly enjoyed was playing the organ at St Davids Cathedral from time to time. Timothy Noon often asked me to accompany the services at the Cathedral when the assistant organist was not available, or they didn't have an organ scholar. I have played for the parish mass at 9.30 and for the main morning service at 11am. Playing for the cathedral was a huge honour, but on an organ such as the one in the cathedral, one must watch Ps and Qs, as it is a very unforgiving beast. The four-manual Harrison and Harrison organ is a beauty, but attention to detail is a must. My playing at the Cathedral from time to time ended when Tim left to take up appointment at Liverpool Cathedral, and I never got to know Tim's successor, although I performed at the St David's Cathedral Festival some years ago and met him then. He seemed a nice guy. I almost forgot, but I also 'helped' at the Cathedral by singing bass in the choir. It was a commitment that only lasted for about 3 months, and I cannot say that it was an overly enjoyable experience. I was well known in the cathedral, yet there was an air of superiority there, and it was extremely difficult to feel part of the group, or indeed accepted. They did not engage in much conversation, and I found them very much gathered into cliques. I did make a mistake accepting this because the commitment was huge, and it meant I could not play the organ for some weeks. My time at the Cathedral, due to my organ playing commitments elsewhere, was limited, and I was attending the bare minimum of what was required. I do hasten to add, however, that despite being eligible for the lay-clerk fees, I never claimed them. I was happy to help when I did and for as long as I was able, and it didn't feel that accepting the fees was the correct thing to do. I think it is fair at this point to mention that this fits in with the recruitment and retention issues that beleaguer many choirs and groups, as 'newbies' often find it extremely difficult to be welcomed and accepted as they ought to be. There is a stiff upper lip reticence about us Brits, and therefore retention is an ever-growing problem, as we do not seem to ever learn the need to be wholly inclusive in groups. However, I digress…

I have, on several occasions, accompanied performers making recordings. I have also played for backing music to wedding videos, and I have also composed Preces and Responses, although again, composition is something I dislike. It doesn't flow, and I was never destined to be a composer – I will leave that to the people who love it and enjoy it and are good at it. Some of the little sacred music I have composed has been performed by the choirs of St Fin Barre's Cathedral in Cork, and I believe at Salisbury Cathedral. I guess that is some sort of achievement, but it is not something I would do in a heartbeat. In fact, I hated the little bits of composition I had to do for my degree and other examinations, and as for writing for quartets and sextets as so forth, no thanks. In recent years I wrote a piece in conjunction with Jenny Nicholson, a local composer from Fishguard, entitled 'Your love surrounds me.' I have played it on several of my live piano shows on social media. Do listen out for it.

'Helping out' is a difficult thing to do when one is a professional musician because there is an expectation to do it on a 'thank you very much' basis. To be honest, this can be insulting to a top-class musician, yet organisations in small localities lack the funds, so it is a difficult balance to maintain, or to get right. For me, it becomes an issue when people *expect* you to play or conduct for nothing. I have performed more events free of charge than I have ever charged for, but when it is *assumed* that one does, *then* I do have a problem with this. I have never charged any charity to conduct, so all my concerts at St David's Hall and other similar venues have been free of charge, but I do negotiate a hotel stay out of it.

I have always weighed up the 'bigger picture' carefully, and if the event is good for my CV, then being paid for it is not that important. I have, unfortunately, on a few occasions, played for weddings and haven't been paid. This really annoys me. I always ask for the fee to be payable on the day, preferably before a note is sounded. The usual excuse is that it was forgotten, and I will get it tomorrow or the next day. I have had a few occasions where the fee never materialised, and I know full well that they never had any intention of paying it. This is **not** how you treat a fellow human being who has been good enough to give of their time and skill to make a wedding day memorable. It saddens me, and it also dents my faith in human nature. It is often very difficult to remember that one is a Christian! Having said all of this, it is very important to help people, because you will be thought highly of for doing it, and if you can make somebody's day brighter, then it has been worth it. It's the little gestures that often make the biggest impression on individuals.

In 1994 I was appointed Musical Director of Whitland Male Choir, but I only wanted the appointment as a 'help out' commitment, and I gave them a year from the outset. Having been a member of the choir back in the 80s, I was shocked at the choir I inherited, the standard had dropped so much, it was as if I was standing in front of a different choir.

We had some great times together, although the choir and I were often at loggerheads because of their need to drink before a concert. To me, this is a no-no and I have zero tolerance, but almost 30% of the choir would sneak out a watering hole near to the concert venue and sink many pints.

In the spring of 1996 (yes, I was still there!) I conducted them at Jeffreyston Church. A good number of the choir were frankly sloshed coming onto stage, and their performance was far less than par shall we say. There were comments from the audience that they could smell the alcohol on the members as they sang, and to add insult to injury one member tripped whilst walking in, and also dropped his music all over the floor (they had folders to sing one new piece), but lo and behold many members had far too many pieces in the folder. Frankly, the concert was an embarrassment, and for me, the final straw. The chairman received my resignation the very next morning, with immediate effect. It can take weeks and weeks of hard work training a choir, and then it can be blown out of the water in a few minutes. My reputation as a musician, organist, and teacher as well as a conductor was not going to be ruined by a choir that liked to beer-swill at every opportunity.

I could not bring myself to go back to them, and I never regretted it. They didn't deserve a dedicated conductor, and I certainly had no tolerance for boozers to that extent. Shame on them I say. Before I end this chapter, I will share with you a couple of humorous stories, all of which are true.

In 1990 I was asked to play for a Harvest thanksgiving in a Church in Carmarthenshire. I was running late and got myself into a bit of a tizz, so I was rushing. It was dark, and when I stepped out of the car I stood in something soft..... Ooh dear, some dog or animal had suffered a bit of a problem! My shoes were discarded by the car, and I walked up to the church and down the nave in socks, and brightly coloured ones as I hate black socks!!

*Dream, Believe, Achieve*

The second story brings me to 1994 and I was conducting a concert in Caerphilly, guest conducting a combined concert of ladies' choirs in the castle. During the singing of '*The rhythm of life*' a lady in the front row lost her false teeth – the whole top set firing out of her mouth like a cannon ball from a cannon!! It was a very humorous moment, and I often think that Sir Tom Jones has ladies throw their knickers at him, and I have false teeth! Says it all really. The lady in question simply bent down, picked up her missing molars from the grass and popped them back in!!!

The final story is of an organ recital I gave in Swansea back in the 1990s. It was in a chapel, and it was a dark winter's night. I played a demanding programme, and about halfway through I was playing Buxtehude's Chaconne, prelude, and fugue, and whilst holding a chord on 'tutti,' I blew the chapel's electrics. We were plummeted into complete darkness. I could not even see my hand in front of my face. The recital ended with a whimper, and everybody being ushered out by torch light and candles hastily sought from the vestry! Although it wasn't my fault per se, I was wholly embarrassed. I was never asked back!! In fact, I was blamed for the calamity, but in reality, it was their electrics that could not withstand the draw of the organ. Going back many years when I lived at home, I performed at the English congregational church, known as 'the cong.' The organ was a very small, two-manual tracker. I had to play Bach's Toccata and Fugue in D Minor, and for some reason, a week prior, when I was rehearsing, the cord connection to bellows snapped. The organist at 'the cong,' the late John Bennett was flapping around and was most upset that I had 'broken the organ,' I took little notice of his little tantrum, as he knew very little anyway, was a hopeless organist, and was a right fanny! He was camper than a Christmas tree, and his opinion was not required.

## Chapter 9
Funerals & Weddings

A staple of an organist's career is playing for funerals. Weddings are much fewer and far between, and sometimes tend to be a lot more hassle. Since I began playing the organ in 1980, I have played for thousands of funerals. Yes, you have read correctly – thousands!

I have played for the parish funerals in every residency I have been appointed to, but in 1991 I was appointed Organist at Parc Gwyn Crematorium in Narberth, and back in those days there was no crematorium at Aberystwyth or Llanelli. It was nothing to play for 10-14 funerals a day. The only downside of the job was that it was a three-way share, so I only covered the duty for the months of March, June, September and December. December at Parc Gwyn was a crazy month, and each day could see a minimum of 12 services, and often more every day. The superintendent and registrar at the crematorium was the Revd Elwyn John, BD (Hons). F.Inst.BCA., PGCE.,

Elwyn was a character, and well known in the county, and often it was difficult to take him as a man of the cloth. He had a wicked sense of humour, and he loved a tipple, like the best of us. Elwyn had many careers during his working life; he had worked as a telephone operator in the old Haverfordwest exchange, School teacher of English and RE., He had also been Congregational minister of Narberth and Templeton United reformed churches.

I spent from 1991-1998 at the Crematorium, and the months I was not working I was teaching music and performing professionally. My organ colleagues at the crematorium were Miss Eluned Jones, an ex-schoolteacher and Mrs Peggy Morgan, LLCM(TD) ALCM.,

Being a crematorium organist is varied and challenging on times, simply because you can be faced with any musical request. Families always selected their loved one's favourite piece of music, and as organists we had to play it, either on entry or exit, so we had to be able to play pretty much everything at sight. All denominations used the crematorium, and as such we had to play hymns from numerous hymnals, including the ones used by the Jehovah Witnesses. During my tenure I had several requests that were, in my opinion, not very suitable. One was *'smoke gets in your eyes,'* and the other was *'The entertainer'* by Scott Joplin. In such instances I always insisted that the minister announce this fact to the congregation, because if he did not, I wouldn't half have some peculiar looks as people filed out!

Having already enjoyed many years as a church organist, I knew many of the vicars and ministers that attended the crematorium to officiate at the services, and many were very regular indeed, so were making a fortune in fees!

Funerals from the back of beyond, way in the hills of North Pembrokeshire and into Ceredigion, especially non-conformist services, attracted crowds in their hundreds. The non-conformist services would see a full chapel and many standing outside. There would be a row of anything up to 10 ministers standing in the front, each one of them poised to take part in some shape or form. The officiating minister would often ramble on and on, and once the entourage started, these funerals always overran their time slot, and sometimes considerably so. They would bark and bellow, firstly in Welsh and then repeat everything in English. When the hymns were announced they would read through the whole verse, which was so unnecessary. The reason why they were so long-winded was because here was a captive audience. In their own country chapel week by week, their congregation would only be about 5 members, so these ministers would take great advantage of having several hundred hearing their voice. Many of them were old-style preachers, who were not far short from the 'fire and brimstone' brigade. It was rather funny to be honest, but on times it was extremely frustrating, especially if it was a hectic day.

I remember one old vicar, he must have been about 100, and I don't think his surplice had seen an iron since the day he retired. He was obviously somebody the family knew well. I mentioned earlier about sell-by dates, and bless him, his had long expired. He shuffled in on two sticks, trying to read the burial sentences. He got to the rostrum and from the book he had with him, he started conducting a burial at sea service. The funeral director hastily corrected him, and he fumbled some more and pressed the committal button, and the curtain took the coffin from view, even before he had said anything of substance. It really was cringeworthy. Having said this, however, some ministers were very highly regarded, and two locals spring to mind: Revd Geoffrey Eynon from Wolfscastle and the Revd Huw George from Maenchlog/Llandissilio, who both always conducted a very sincere and well thought out service. I also remember with much fondness, the late Canon

Hamer from Narberth. Long retired, he still had all his faculties and conducted a very good funeral service, and I guess the little bit of money helped to supplement a rather poor pension. Canon Hamer was married to a piano teacher, and we often had little chats about pupils and the like.

There were lots of funny stories I could share with you, so I will tell you one other. A local, Pembrokeshire funeral director arrived early with a brand-new ghetto-blaster. It was all singing, all dancing machine. The policy of the crematorium was that any device such as this must be operated by the funeral director, rather than the responsibility being on the crematorium staff, and that was a good idea, because when the whole thing became a 'balls up,' we couldn't be blamed for it. The funeral gathering was very large, and this player was placed upstairs on the gallery, on the wooden ledge, overlooking the main chapel below. The funeral director had already boasted about the fact it was remote controlled. The end of the service came, and everybody was due to listen to a recording of '*My Way,*' by Frank Sinatra. The funeral director walked slowly from the back of the chapel towards the front, and I could see him fumbling with the remote in his hand, and the next thing I saw was lots of people jumping out of their skin as the Owen Money radio from BBC radio Wales jingle belted out on full volume!!

It was an awesome output, and the funeral director got frazzled by the machine he didn't know how to operate, and it got louder and louder. I knew '*My way*' well and made a split-second decision that we couldn't put up with this embarrassment a second longer. I pushed my way from the organ stool, through the 4-deep crowd, and hit the plug to off. I went back to the organ and played the piece, albeit without being sung.

I chuckled about this for some time, and it certainly brought the funeral director down to earth with a bit of a bang to say the least! It was a bit of karma because he was a big-headed old bugger! It couldn't have happened to a nicer chap, but I did feel for the family as having their favourite piece played on an organ is not the same as having it sung by Frank Sinatra!

Oh, final one (I knew you wanted more…) The coffin arrived, the family gathered behind, the vicar started his lines, and in they came. Everybody was looking at each other, as if the whole lot of them were concerned about something. It didn't become apparent until the vicar leaned on the lectern, casually, and started to speak about the late Doris. The problem was that it was a Raymond that was deceased, and it transpired that the vicar had entered with the wrong funeral, blaming the fact he had forgotten his watch and was running early. Surely, he would have realised something wasn't quite right when he didn't recognise anybody present? What a 'plonker' he was. It was very amusing to be fair, something you see on the television. The family were very gracious and had to wait about 10 minutes until their correct vicar showed up (who was running late). It was like a scene from a 'carry on' film.

I had to leave the crematorium shortly after my daughter Jessica was born in 1998. Financially, we found it increasingly difficult, and being a professional musician wasn't bringing the money in to sustain everything. Gail and I had a good life, and now with a new baby to support, I had to think of extra ways to earn money. That is, however, not relevant to this book, so I will leave it there. I will say, however, that the crematorium was managed by a 'joint committee,' made up of county councillors serving the three counties as they were then of Pembrokeshire, Carmarthenshire and Cardiganshire. Most of them were old 'duffers' that had little or no interest in the crematorium, but they were interested in the expenses, and the so-called kudos; we've all met these sorts, especially in local government, where most of them are full of self-interest, and are basically less than honest!

An incident that caused me much angst was when Eluned Jones decided to retire as organist. I lobbied hard for Peggy Morgan and myself to be the only two organists, as alternate months for me would have been a perfect role.

The crematorium had 'always' had 3 organists, so they saw no need to change it (another example of not being willing to embrace new ideas). The post was advertised, and I was asked to sit on the interviewing panel, to which I agreed initially. Peggy Morgan was not interested in the slightest. I saw the applications, many of which were from qualified musicians, of associate and/or Licentiate standard. These individuals stood out from the crowd in the interview and were great candidates. However, my feedback counted for nothing, as they appointed a chap who was not a qualified musician, save for a grade 6 Trinity college piano grade. I was furious, and when I demanded to know the reason, it transpired that this chap's partner had a father who was a county councillor, and a member of the management committee, and clearly strings had been pulled, which was nepotism at its best! This sort of thing happens all the time, and it really ought to be made a criminal offence. I demanded a meeting with the full committee, which they agreed to, and I asked some very potent and direct questions as to why they passed over, qualified people and yet appointed through nepotism. I was told that I was out of order to be questioning it. I really ought to have gone further into this, as it was so very wrong. I have no faith whatsoever in most county councillors, they are in it for their own ends, and many of them are as crooked as a dog's hind leg! The appointee in question was a real gent, and he and I got on very well, and I had no problem with him personally, but I did have a problem with the process of his appointment. We see it happening all too often, don't we? There is corruption in the corridors of many public sector organisations. I am a Fellow of the society of Crematorium Organists (FCSO) and perhaps one day I might get another such opportunity; they were happy times, and a great honour to bring joy through music at a family's unhappiest time.

I was very sad to leave the crematorium. I had made good friendships there, and if the job was full-time, it would have been a perfect place to spend the rest of my working life. It was doing a job I could do with my eyes closed, and it was so easy; There was no stress, and Elwyn was a fantastic boss, and it was like one big family. Elwyn John, 'the boss,' hobbled here and there by officiating at funerals and weddings, and because I could find my way around an organ rather proficiently, I was booked to play most of these services with him. Elwyn had a certain way about him that endeared him to everybody. He was a bit of a scallywag, but everybody loved him for it, he was human after all. Over a period of about 10 years, I have played in most chapels in the area where he was booked to officiate.

The same was true with weddings. He was heavily involved at Tabernacle Chapel in Narberth, and I played for several weddings there. It was a good little earner on the side, and he kept the work coming my way. Elwyn would crack jokes and have the congregation rolling with laughter. He once told a story about a former Rector of Narberth, the Revd Hugh Thomas. Hugh had a very unfortunate voice; he spoke in a monotone and had a very loud delivery. In fact, he would bore a glass eye to sleep!

He told the congregation of the time Hugh Thomas was preaching in his chapel for a Harvest thanksgiving, and two old ladies at the back of the chapel started talking during his sermon. The one lady, he said, was terribly deaf, and misheard the other woman when she said, "He bawls like a bull!" The other lady responded in a Pembrokeshire drawl, "'ave he?"

The wedding party were creased with laughter, and Elwyn very often came out with such things. I have always kept in touch with Elwyn and his wife Margaret to this day, and they don't live terribly far from my parents. I very much appreciate vicars and ministers being 'ordinary,' because they are genuine. Far too many clergy feel the need to be sombre and always dress in black. Why? God has a sense of humour, so why don't they?

I have played for weddings as a guest organist throughout the area, and I remember playing for a service in about 1989, and the bride didn't show. The church was full, and eventually the vicar and best man were able to contact the bride, and she had jilted him. The poor vicar had to make an announcement to the congregation, after he had talked to the groom, who left by another door via the vestry. My first thoughts were, *I hope I am getting paid.* I'm not a charity you know, and I had already played for 30 minutes or more. Thankfully I was paid.

Weddings have always been a mixed bag as far as etiquette is concerned. When I was organist at St Mary's in Pembroke, invariably a good number of the male guests were drunk! I have also experienced a little bit of this at St Katharine's in Milford Haven. Most weddings that take place in church are held there purely for the backdrop. These people don't know how to conduct themselves inside a scared place of worship, and they show little respect. I have also played at a wedding, and when I arrived, I witnessed guests (male of course) urinating up against gravestones and drinking cans of lager. This was totally disrespectful, and sums everything up for me as to the way society is heading.

Currently, it is very costly to keep a church open for worship. There is what's called the *ministry share,* which is what churches must pay to central funds in Cardiff, to pay for clergy and their pensions. St Katharine's in Milford Haven must find £70,000 a year just to fund the ministry share, and this is before any heating, lighting or insurances and other associated costs. Therefore, clergy invite people to donate if they so wish, as the money is very much needed. I often leave the church after all the guests have gone, and all too often I see what amounts to a couple of quid on the money plate; what an insult this is. The parish church is just seen as a commodity, a convenience to people, for them to look good in photographs of their 'big day.' This saddens me to be honest, because they have no idea how to behave, or how to treat the building with respect, and the very fact that the building is 'used and abused' in such a way makes me shudder.

I have played in many hundreds of weddings both locally and further afield. I enjoy a good wedding, but not many really listens to the organ anymore, nor do they on a Sunday. It is just a familiar sound that was always been there, and it provides background music for them, and I appreciate that this is what the organ preludes are meant to do. There are occasions when I get annoyed by the volume of the talking, but most of the time I must allow it to drift over my head, although it is disrespectful to the organist, who is **not** using this time as practise!

When the Venerable Dennis Wight was Vicar of Dale with St Brides and Marloes on the Pembrokeshire coast, I was engaged as organist for all the weddings that happened in those parishes. St Brides' church, dedicated to St Bridget, was the favourite venue at which to hold a wedding, with its wonderful backdrop of the ocean, and Dennis loved to tell people that the next Parish as the crow flies over the sea, was New York.

One occasion, I had a wedding there in the morning, and then I had to rush over to play for a wedding at St Mary's in Whitland at 2pm, only to rush back to Dale for another wedding at 4.30pm. Following this I went back to the wedding reception of the Whitland wedding as my daughter was a bridesmaid, and it was a close family friend. I was saddened to learn that the happy couple who married at St Bride's church that day suffered a tragedy whilst on honeymoon when the new husband was killed in a freak surfing accident. That is tragedy beyond comprehension.    I very much enjoyed working with Dennis – a straightforward, no nonsense priest.

The most weddings I have played for have been at St Katharine's Church, Milford Haven. There are usually several weddings each year, as the church is very much at the heart of the community of Milford, plus it has a very long aisle, which is wonderfully conducive for the bride and her dad to make a grand entrance.

The advent of the COVID-19 pandemic has thwarted such a lot of people's plans, and weddings have been hit hard. I didn't have any wedding bookings in 2020, and so far for 2021, they are being pushed back and back, with bookings in the diary, but I am not sure if they will happen. Churches are prohibited from having singing in any service, which I think is ridiculous, as everybody has been inoculated and are wearing face masks. I am really concerned that my church choir, consisting mostly of elderly people, and now we are into the second year of no singing, that it will be difficult, if not impossible, to get back to where we were pre-COVID.

I had a conversation with one member recently, and I could sense an apprehension developing, and of course when you are in your late seventies or eighties, a year can make a marked difference to your health and confidence. I do hope that everything will work out for the best, but the pandemic of COVID-19 has changed this world, and not for the better.

I hope and pray that the choir at St Katharine's and St Peter's will resume exactly as it was previously because we have all put a lot of effort into it, and it is a very enjoyable hour on a Wednesday evening. The members all enjoy the choir, and it is never anything heavy, other than to look through the following Sunday's service music, and perhaps a special anthem for when the occasion dictates. Choir rehearsals last 60 minutes, and I make sure that it is fun, but at the same time purposeful. I will probably have to think of a recruitment drive in the not-too-distant future, but I am not holding out much hope of attracting recruits. Nobody seems to want to join a church choir nowadays as they fear the commitment. I did touch upon this in other parts of the book, but church choir recruitment really suffered when sports clubs introduced their training sessions on a Sunday. There is not even the slightest possibility that we can compete! There is much reticence with adults as well, even committed church goers, and it is always 'leave it to somebody else' mentality, but of course if everybody said this, we would not have a choir at all, in any church. I remember a time when church choirs were thriving, with the stalls full to bursting, but sadly this is past tense. The church choirs as we knew them are, in the majority of churches, a thing of the past.

*Dream, Believe, Achieve*

## Chapter 10
*The Gild of Freemen and the Town Council*

One of the earliest known charters of Haverfordwest, of about 1213, decreed that a man who dwelt in the town of Haverford for a year and a day without challenge, shall be 'free.'

A Burgess of Haverfordwest, of which I am one, enjoyed the rare privilege of being able to sell his burgage, the standard unit of land without the Lord's consent, or if he could hand it on to the heir. As time went by, Freeman of Haverfordwest were admitted by birth or by servitude, that is, having served an apprenticeship with the freemen for seven years. Amongst the privileges of the Freeman was a right to graze the common land at Portfield, which extended to some 600 acres or thereabouts. Under the Portfield enclosure act of 1838, 174 acres of land including the town racecourse were allocated to the mayor aldermen and burgesses for a place of recreation exercise for the neighbouring population, and 251 acres of land were given to trustees for the benefit of the Freeman of the town the annual income therefore being distributed between the Freemen.

As time continued, the opportunities for admission by servitude declined, although freemen continued to be admitted under the hereditary principle, i.e., the son or grandson of a Freeman could apply to be admitted as a Freeman once he had reached the age of 18. Following various changes in statutes relating to local government, candidates

**143**

for admission can now be either male or female. Although the Haverfordwest Freeman trust exists for the benefit of the Freeman of the town, it is not the trust which appoints new Freeman but the chairman of the local authority which is Pembrokeshire County Council.

In 1973 the Gild (and this is the correct spelling) of Freeman of Haverfordwest was established as it was felt that the Freeman of the borough might lose their identity with the abolishment of the Haverfordwest borough council by the local government act of 1972, and the transfer of responsibility for keeping the Freeman's role and for admitting new Freeman, to the District Council of the day. The day-to-day affairs of the Gild are managed by a court of wardens but the ultimate authority rests with the body of Freeman and burgesses at their annual general meeting. The annual general meeting of the Guild of Freeman of Haverfordwest takes place on the 1st Saturday of October each year, and this is followed by an evening banquet and the Sunday morning service at St Martin's church which is the only one of the three main town churches built within the Old Town walls, but of course, St Thomas' Church is now closed and sold as a private dwelling, although the graveyard remains public.

I was very fortunate a few years ago, 2013 to be exact, to be appointed a Burgess of Haverfordwest, number 103 on the roll, and within the statute of 1215, it states that the burgesses are appointed from 'persons of repute who have rendered outstanding service to the town.' I am not too sure if that word 'repute' could be misconstrued, but it does genuinely mean individuals of worthy repute, so I must have done something write to be deemed eligible for this honour! The burgesses do not receive any financial benefit or reward although they do help to promote the interests of the Freeman and partake in a meaningful local discussion for the benefit of the town itself. The badge of the Gild depicts a trading ship, indicating the maritime associations of the town, it sails bearing the Prince of Wales feathers to commemorate the granting of a charter of incorporation to the town by Edward Prince of Wales in 1479.

Whilst I was very honoured to become a Burgess of Haverfordwest, I have only attended a small handful of annual general meetings, and the reason being that every year, without fail, the whole Gild weekend is the same without exception from the previous year. The Saturday evening banquet is a black-tie affair, always held at Wolfscastle country hotel, and the entertainment that is provided is somewhat moot to say the least. I will share a funny tale with you regarding the 'entertainment.' A few years ago, when my daughter Jess accompanied me to the banquet, because Gail was home, unwell in bed at that time, and I thought we had better attend, to show one's face as it were. Jess and I sat opposite a lady freeman, who is a former teacher at Sir Thomas Picton school, who is something of a 'tonic' shall we say. The 'entertainment' came on after the three-course meal, prior to the speeches, and it was… shall we say, far less than I would deem acceptable, and clearly this lady felt the same way because as the applause died away, she looked directly at me and in a very loud voice declared, "Ooh, weren't they dreadful!" at which point many people turned in their seats to look at her. Whilst her comment was hilarious, it was also extremely embarrassing, and as they were a singing act, I think she thought that I would concur, which I did of course, but I didn't want to make any public indication – I do have some limitations to what is and is not acceptable to say in public. I must say that I have come across this sort of situation many times throughout my career, and I'm not sure what motivates such people to perform in public, when it is clear that they are not up to the job. I think it must be a somewhat distorted ideology that they are good, or perhaps somebody has promoted them with much praise, somewhat ill-conceived, however. I am totally in favour of children 'having a go,' but when adults perform in public and they are less than good, I have a problem with it; once again the "it'll do," philosophy.

I feel somewhat strongly that the Gild weekend ought to be varied, because frankly it is boring and a waste of one's valuable time. Even the hymns in the service are the same year on year, the readers are usually the same, and so it continues. Even tradition can be varied, because at the end of the day, *variety* IS the spice of life. The Gild is managed by a court of wardens, many of whom are elderly, and there is this acceptance isn't there of keeping everything the same; traditional, but everything must have slight variance to maintain interest and indeed momentum, and to facilitate the interest of the younger generations.

As I said, I am extremely proud to be a burgess, and when you next walk around the racecourse, which is adjacent to the Haverfordwest cricket club, you will appreciate a little of the history behind these two pieces of land which are located on both sides of the Dale Road.

The burgess declaration ceremony, was, as I said, in June 2013, and two other 'people of repute' were admitted as burgesses at the same time; Joyce Wonacott, long-serving town councillor, past deputy Mayor, Mayor and Sheriff, and Mr Glan Phillips, FRCS., retired Orthopaedic consultant surgeon at Withybush General Hospital. A year or so after my installation, Mr Robert Nesbitt, MA., former Head of the English department at Milford Comprehensive school, was installed as a Burgess. Robert's wife Gill was a founder member of my choir. I knew Robert well, and his sense of humour, very similar to mine, meant that we always got on very well.

A year after, my good friend Mike Davies, who wrote the foreword of this book) was admitted as a burgess, which in my opinion was long overdue. I would like to mention at this point, and I am able to now, knowing that the nominations were unsuccessful. On two separate occasions I nominated Mike for a Queen's honour and on both occasions he was unsuccessful. This somewhat dented my faith in the honours system, simply because Mike has done more for Pembrokeshire and local and national charities than anybody else I know, and yet there are people in Pembrokeshire, who shall remain nameless of course, who received MBE's 'willy-nilly.' I am convinced that it really is *who* you know. I know of people who have been awarded the MBE 'for services to music,' and they can't even play a bloody instrument, but when you look carefully at their circle of friends, the mist begins to clear, and one can see how the application was approved! No wonder it dents faith in the system.

It's funny isn't it, how this, like so many other things in life is achieved by *who you know*. As I said to you earlier, luck and I do not share a harmonious relationship, and if I was in a marching band, I'd be on the piano! My grandfather too was unlucky, he started his business in 1931, worked hard at building it up, and worked for 70 years. Do you know what he was worth when he died? Nothing, and he still owed for the handcart! Whilst this is, of course, a joke, it sums up perfectly how my luck has worked over the years. Everything I have achieved has been through sheer determination and hard work, and never have I been handed anything on a plate. I am proud of this fact, and another reason for me perhaps not being as lucky as some other people is because I am not a 'yes man,' or a 'Brownnoser,' unlike so many other people today who climb their way up the greasy pole by knowing the right people, or by being 'expedient' to management. I speak the truth, offend or please, and I have never expected anybody to like me through misrepresentation. Take me as I am or not at all is the mantra we need nowadays. I have little faith or respect for such ideologies, and many leaders in today's organisations are contemptuous in the extreme.

In addition to my musical abilities, I have always enjoyed administration and public speaking. I am a reasonable orator, and I am not fazed by speaking in front of hundreds of people. Since moving to Haverfordwest in 1995, I wanted to become part of the town council, but my musical career and family took precedence, plus I was not local, and felt that it was probably necessary to be local, born and bred 'Harfat' to be eligible.

Some years ago, I did some research into the possibility, and I was surprised to find out that I could indeed stand for election as a town councillor. There was a vacancy in the priory ward, which incidentally is the largest ward in the town. My name was put forward and the campaign started. Gail and I walked many miles putting campaign letters through hundreds of homes and speaking to people on the doorsteps. Not everybody was friendly, but they just hear the word *council* and they automatically jumped to a conclusion that I was running for election to the local authority of Pembrokeshire County council. Heaven forbid; I might be keen, but I'm not a masochist! After about 3 weeks of heavy campaigning, the election took place, and I was standing against 3 other candidates. I didn't think for one moment that I stood a chance, but I won a landslide victory, and duly elected as a councillor for priory ward, to serve the ancient township of Haverfordwest.

The next day I attended the town clerk and took the declaration of office. I was then known as Cllr Richard Stephens. I had many things I wanted to bring to the table and to try and encourage change for the better, but soon on I realised that it was going to be far more difficult than I first anticipated. Many of the older councillors had served on there since Charles Dickens was in the books chart! Their draconian thinking was protuberant, and it was always look for a reason to say no to something, rather looking positively and saying 'yes.' By nature, I am an extremely optimistic person with the metaphorical glass always half full, rather than empty, but many councillors couldn't see positivity in anything. It was a case of *'this is how it has been since 1936, and I see little point in changing it now...'*

My first term in office was under the chairmanship of Mayor and admiral of the port, Cllr Roy Thomas, JP., I never worked him out to be honest, and I think he knew how to work the system well for his own ends. It soon became clear that there existed several cliques within the chamber, and I always knew that politics, albeit local, was something of a game to be played. Despite bringing much to the table, I only managed to get 'no parking' lines placed in Augustine way for Pamela Harries, and even then, it was nothing but a fight.

The town council, in my opinion, was all too often about pomp and ceremony, and they revelled in it. I am a great believer in tradition and pomp where necessary, but not when it is self-promoting above all else. I suggested at a meeting of the full council that we be seen to support all the local hostelries and hotels in the area when we organised any buffet or reception. To my mind this was the fair and equitable way to be, but of course, a councillor was also a trustee of a certain club in town, hence they always had the functions there. I didn't see that this was fair.

The second year there was a change of Mayor to Cllr Sue Murray. To give Sue due credit she was a go-getter, a feisty individual but tended to be downright rude and antagonistic. She was as blunt as a spoon and spoke to grown adults like dirt. I didn't like her it has to be said, and I also felt that the council was too hierarchal, with 'senior' councillors having much of the influence, and we 'junior' councillors being overridden with a worked-out voting system, called the 'scratch back' system. There was one or two councillors who always made this difference between longer serving and newer councillors, and I challenged this at one meeting. As far as I was concerned, whilst we may not have had as much local government experience, we were professionals in our own fields, and we won elections fair and square to become a Town Councillor, **not** a junior councillor. I berated them and I'd like to think they saw the error of their ways.

By nature, I can be a challenger, especially if I know the opposition is wrong. I am like a dog with a bone and will not accept 'bullshit' in any shape or form. It never ceases to amaze me in all walks of life such as employment, organisations etc, that simply because someone is of a higher position, they think that they are always right, and that their ideas are somehow superior. I hate this intensely! There's a lot of these people around, and people with opinions that know nothing about what they are talking. I do value another opinion, but there is an old saying that my headmaster used to say, *'empty vessels make the most noise.'* Make of that what you will.

Towards the end of Cllr Sue Murray's year in office, discussions were being had, sometimes covertly, as to who would be nominated to what position. Cllr Alan Buckfield was the deputy Mayor, and so he would have natural progression to Mayor, although the vote could still have gone against him. When the time came to vote, it was clear that he was going to be Mayor, and somehow, he managed to persuade me to stand as deputy Mayor. My nomination was proposed by Cllr Peter Iles. I was elected unanimously. I must be honest and say that I felt very inexperienced to become deputy Mayor, deputy chair of the council, but the rest had faith in me, so I was certainly up for the job. I am not too sure what my expectations were, but it didn't turn out anything like what I was expecting. I had expected to be a year in training, learning the ropes as it were to take the helm the following May. Instead, I was simply a stand-in for the mayor, and this was usually at events he didn't like, or simply didn't want to go to. I went to many events, sometimes as much as twice a week, and usually I would go to any concert. I attended many gala concerts in the Cathedral as it was customary to invite all the local Mayors. We were all sitting in the front three rows in the Cathedral looking like bejewelled manakins out of Rembrandts' window! I did find it a little disconcerting because I don't 'do small talk,' and there is a good deal of this required. However, we battled through, and one event I enjoyed more than most was being a VIP guest at the Royal Welch Fusiliers army base at Brawdy for a gala evening. The concert was a military band, and they were outstanding. I did enjoy that evening it must be said.

Being a town councillor is the only role I have done which did not overly attract Gail's support. Gail is a very straight, uncomplicated individual who likes to always have feet firmly on the ground. The certain amount of 'bullshit' that comes with such a role was not for her, although she always attended events with me, supporting me as opposed to the council. Many of the events were like pulling teeth, and the Radio Pembrokeshire awards night was one such occasion. A fancy meal and then speeches, it went on and on, and then the nominations and presentations. It was like the BAFTAs, only at Milford Haven in a marquee on the docks.

The council observed strict 'protocol,' which sometimes was a step too far, and was often preposterous in so much that it mattered above all else. Who would walk behind so-in-so and all of that jazz, and there was always a big scene made if a councillor was in the wrong position. Did it really matter? The town was falling apart around us, and here we were walking like some stuffy clowns through the middle of the town, expecting people to be gracious. There are more important things for a council to do than to look the part, bedecked in their finery. I used to say, 'there's more to being a councillor you know than dressing up for it.' Don't get me wrong I am the first to uphold tradition, but when it came before anything else, I have a problem with it.

I really struggled being deputy Mayor with all the 'bull' and nonsense, as well as inter-quarrelling, and to my mind they had lost totally, the vision of doing good for the town and its people. They would argue over the Christmas lights, and penny pinch here and there. It was relentless, and Alan was rather weak as a mayor, and sadly, nobody liked him which didn't help the cause. He was a bit of a strange one I must admit, but I put that down to him being a pearly king! I asked to attend the chamber when local organisations came to visit the council offices, this was denied initially, although I pressed hard on the issue, and eventually he relented. I wanted to learn to do the best job possible the following year, not just because one must do one's best in such a role for the constituents, but your fellow councillors, or certainly some of them, would rip you to shreds if you did something wrong. However, many organisations visited the chamber and Mayor's parlour without my knowing about it, and everything was held during the working hours of a day, so it was difficult for those of us in employment to make ourselves available.

On one occasion when I deputised for the mayor at full meeting of the council, these old duffers had a shock. I have had vast experience on committees and chaired at national level in Cardiff. I am a firm chairman; clear, concise, I do not allow any digression from the agenda, and I insist that all discussions are relevant and worthy. I had to bang the gavel on a couple of occasions and call the chamber to order. I also gave a councillor fair warning for removal from the chamber if his attitude to a fellow councillor did not improve. The mayor (or deputy in this case) has a lot of power within the council chamber, and that meeting which I chaired was one of the most effective and efficient council meetings ever experienced in recent years. There was no bullshit that night allowed to waffle its way around the table!

I did not, however, go on to become Mayor. I didn't feel that I had been given the necessary support to do the job to the best of my ability, and I know my personality only too well, so it was best to withdraw. In fact, I was so disillusioned, and I knew, that in her heart, Gail hated the council and everything it stood for, and when discussions were had at home about my daughter becoming my Mayoress, I realised that it was a no-go. This is not, however, the reason I withdrew.

I withdrew over something you might think is rather trivial, but it was the final straw for me. I had won two raffles in the Haverfordwest business circle draw. One was a mug with the Haverfordwest business circle emblazoned upon it, and the other was a Haverfordwest Yarn bombers mug, which was gratifyingly colourful.

I was very pleased with my win, and I proudly put a photograph on social media, and thanked the business circle. I also stated that these mugs would sit proudly on my desk. I got on terribly well with the business circle, and in chamber I was a staunch defender of them.

That was sufficient for Cllr Roy Thomas to pull me aside and tell me I was 'out of order,' because the council cannot be "seen to support the business circle." I certainly voiced a difference of opinion to him at the picton centre that night. Here was a hard-working band of business owners, doing so much for their businesses and the town traders, and this is the view of a former Mayor and Admiral of the Port. I was flabbergasted and repulsed, and the town clerk received my resignation the next day. As far as I was concerned, this was *not* the attitude required!

The sheriff, good old Cllr Sue Murray, Haverfordwest's answer to Cruella De'ville, decided that she would take exception to my resignation, and she sent me the most awful of text messages, to which I duly retorted, of course! She even had the audacity to come to my home, looking for an argument. Thankfully, Gail was home, and if you think my bite is bad, you've seen nothing until Gail gets going. Even an adder would slide away quicker than a bullet from a gun if Gail started on it. Cllr Murray was sent packing down our drive, with a huge flea in her ear, and told never to tread foot on our premises again. I certainly concurred. She was a right battle-axe, and not a very nice person. There is a saying which I think about often, and it goes like this: *It is nice to be important, but more important to be nice.* This is so true, and many people would do well to learn and inwardly digest this saying!

I do, on occasion, regret that I didn't carry on becoming Mayor of Haverfordwest, simply because it would have appealed to my historical nature, and the office of Mayor and admiral of the Port goes back into the 13th Century. Up until 1972, the Mayor of Haverfordwest had tremendous power and was a high ruler of the township. Alas, it was not meant to be, but despite the ups and downs, I will look at my time there with fondness. I am also proud of the work I did with the graveyard trust. I prepared an in-depth feasibility study and business case to turn the upper part of the Haverfordwest St Martin's cemetery, which was directly under the care of the town council and not the local authority, into a remembrance garden. The area had already been de-consecrated some years previously, and many of the graves in that area were dating back many hundreds of years, with no family remaining of any of the deceased. Part of the in-depth study was to see if any relatives were surviving as their permission was required to remove the headstone, as I wanted to place all headstones around the perimeter wall, and therefore, allowing the lovely rose garden of remembrance to be built in the central area. I worked closely with the Church in Wales authorities in Cardiff, and this is one project I am sorry that I didn't see through to realisation. It was an ambitious, 5-year plan, and I will always take pride in the comprehensive presentation I gave to the council.

Haverfordwest, over the years, has had lots of Mayors, but very few sticks in one's memory for making that difference. The best Mayor that Haverfordwest has ever had (or will have again) was Cllr Mike Davies, and a close second to him was the late Cherie Harvey. Those two people did far and beyond anything ever done before or since, and I salute them both. Cherie was taken from us all too soon from cancer, leaving a husband and young son. Cherie was a brilliant town councillor, but whilst in office she became very poorly, and I was saddened and shocked to learn that the council voted her out of office, simply because she hadn't attended X number of meetings. The woman was terminally ill for goodness' sake, and I was totally shocked at this high-handed attitude; compromise is not a word that many people nowadays have heard of.

Sadly, many town councils as well as local authorities lack vision. They lack the desire to do anything of benefit for their towns, and usually it is down to apathy; "tried that and it didn't work." I will always retort, "well let's look at it differently, and make improvement, and it may well work." Usually a very strange, complicated set of ideologies within the town council chamber!! I certainly do not miss it, although I do regret that I could not do more – I simply was not allowed to.

## Chapter 11
*Richard, the teacher.*

Music is one of those subjects that too many unqualified people teach privately. Musicians achieve about grade 7 and they think they can teach. I wholly disagree with this, and I believe that this is doing an injustice to the student. I did not teach any pupils until I became an associate of the Royal College of Music. It was only then that I felt justified to charge tuition fees. Of course, an unqualified individual can adequately teach a beginner, or some of the early grades, but in my informed opinion, lacks the technical know-how to teach into the senior grades.

My teaching career began in 1991, and very soon I was teaching 40 students each week. I would work at the crematorium during the day and then drive over to my studio in Whitland, and start teaching from 4pm, often finishing at 8pm. During the two months that I was not working at the crematorium I was engaged in training sessions and seminars for the RSCM, and teaching adults during the hours of the working day. I was also local representative for the Victoria College of Music in the mid 90s, so this took up quite a lot of my time. It was a time I enjoyed, and as I was studying for my Open University degree, I had a lot of free time in the day in which to study or catch up with various teaching media.

I taught singing, Piano, and theory, from beginner to diploma level. I have never taught the organ, simply because I am not overly convinced sitting in a cold church is going to be conducive to enjoyment any longer. I spent most of my time between 1980 and 1991 and beyond, in a cold church practising the instrument to death, so the appeal of teaching it simply wasn't in my list of priorities, and I think I would be hard pressed to find any youngsters wanting to take on the might of the pipe organ.

I taught varying college syllabi, depending on the want and need of the student. The music colleges offer different types of approach, some are more geared towards encouragement, with a very friendly approach, whilst others are more formal, and aimed at perhaps the more academic candidate. One college for singers may have far better choice of pieces, or one would have a far better choice of musical theatre songs. There was always a lot to consider, and I taught Trinity College of Music, Associated Board of the Royal Schools of Music, Victoria College of Music and the National College of Music and arts. I also did, on occasion, work through the syllabus of the Guildhall school of Music and drama. I tailored the requirements and desire of the student to what I thought was the best college, best suited to their needs. This philosophy worked, and throughout my 25 years of teaching, I have never had a failure. In fact, 87% of my entrants always passed with distinction at all levels. I am proud of this achievement, and I always strived to make lessons interesting and fun, but I always expected results.

My first pupil was someone who certainly had a pushy mother. We have all met the type, and the kid was standing beside her like a wet weekend and had no intention of speaking. Her mother, a schoolteacher by profession, wanted her daughter to have singing lessons. The young girl was about 10 years old at the time and was used to being around a cluck-hen. Eventually she came into the study, and I failed to get a word out of her. I tried everything, but it was all failing. I played middle C and I wanted her just to sing the open vowel sound of 'Ah.' Following a few attempts of great encouragement, she let out a squawk not dissimilar to the craw of a crow. I was slightly down at heel shall we say, but I persevered, thinking of my £10 for 30 minutes tuition as it was then! She couldn't hold a tune in a bucket. She was so out of tune, the chrome on my bike was showing signs of bubbling! I wanted to do some ear tests to ascertain if she was tone deaf, but thankfully so could distinguish between higher and lower pitched sounds, so there was hope. It took me two lessons to get her to sing Middle C and Middle D to an open vowel, and heaven knows how long it took to achieve the octave, comprising of 8 notes for my non-musical readers. After many weeks, we were ready to begin a very basic song, not much more than a nursery rhyme. Her confidence was growing slightly, so I was now getting the odd titter from her, but it was like pulling teeth!

Her mother was determined that she learn to sing, and I don't think I had a choice in the matter, and it is worth noting that the mother was a scouser, a tougher woman you'd never meet!

To cut a long story short, over the period of the next 7 years or slightly longer, she developed into a lovely soprano, and passed Grade 8 with distinction. It was a long road, but I wanted to share that story with you because I think, looking back, she was my biggest success story. The great shame with this pupil was that as soon as she became rather good, the 'diva' took over, and the quiet child had long gone. I accompanied her at A 'level practical when she played the violin, but my advice, and that of her school music teacher fell upon deaf ears. She developed into one of these kids that think they know better than their teachers. Her class teacher and I spoke at length about this, but she wouldn't heed our advice. If she had, then a pass would have been guaranteed, but as it was, she failed the practical element.

I had many pupils whose parents were pushy, and I had some that used me as a creche facility as they did their shopping trip to Tesco. Several kids would have to stay behind over the next lesson until they were collected, and so Gail would dutifully act as a creche worker until the mother showed up. I put up with this for some considerable time, but then I had to tell the mothers that I was not registered as a child-minding service. They got the point! It's difficult to know what to do for the best in such circumstances because the money was needed, but the being taken advantage of was not.

I had a good number of pupils who were serious singers, and Hilary Riley who studied her LRSM with me was a fine example of a brilliant soprano. She could rattle through arias by Mozart and Handel with ease, and there was Mirelle Ryan, one of the best ranged sopranos I have ever come across. She could hit a top C with great ease, and even go up to an E, also with some considerable ease. Her vocal range was incredible, but sadly she was not overly academic to be able to maintain her theory of music to match the practical, and she certainly did not achieve her fullest potential. Both Mirelle and Hilary were members of my choir, Cantabilé, and they both were also regular soloists with the Haverfordwest Male voice choir. Mirelle and I often sang duets together, and this included several hits from *Phantom of the Opera*.

I taught many other singers, but only ever one male pupil, and that was a young student from Steynton, who wanted to learn the arias from the *Marriage of Figaro*. I had several pupils gain their grade 8 with either a merit or distinction, and a few pupils who gained their LRSM.,

I taught about 40 piano pupils at the peak of my teaching career, and this lasted for over 25 years, until my health started to deteriorate somewhat, and a need to take it a little easier was identified. I suffered from extremely high blood pressure, which thankfully is now improved by medication. At this time, I reduced the number of students I had, but this decision was also facilitated by 9 of them gaining grade 8, and not taking their playing any further due to A 'levels and so forth, so there was a natural cull at this point. I also thought it was the right time to pull the plug on those pupils who you only look forward to seeing the colour of their money each week. Every music teacher can identify with this – what heathens we are!

I kept about 6 pupils on up until about 4 years ago, the crem-de-la crème shall we say, but then I decided to call it a day and retire. I must say, in all sincerity, that I have not missed it one little bit. Pupils were becoming more and more difficult to identify with, and there was a growing disrespect for teachers of any kind. The gap of respect was widening, and being somewhat old-fashioned, I don't like this at all. I do not hold with teachers nowadays being called by their first name in school, and 'high-fiving' students as they walk through the corridor. When I was in high school and indeed prep, you walked on the left in a single file, and heaven forbid if you wavered or messed around. I still don't know the Christian name of many of my teachers, and this is how I prefer it.

Some years ago, I applied for a Head of Music position at Netherwood school in Saundersfoot, a fee-paying, private establishment with a wonderful reputation. I knew two teachers there, and they certainly gave me excellent references. I received an interview, and I was on the cusp of being successful, but then the headmaster (who owned the school) rang me up, full of apologies to say that the music teacher who was retiring had now decided to remain, and as she had given 40 plus years of service to the school, he felt duty-bound to keep her on. I was truly devastated by this, as I had the post almost in the palm of my hand.

This leads me onto another of my 'observations.' I am of firm belief that when it is time to retire then go! Sounds harsh? Good. It's meant to be. Too many people are 'retiring and returning,' claiming large 'handshakes,' often claiming state pension, and then coming back into the same employment to earn almost the same as they did substantively, or at least, very similar. Move aside and allow the younger generation to come through and flourish! Know your sell-by date and move on. I see it in the NHS where old dinosaurs, who ought to have been long extinct, return to their inflated-salary positions, and on many occasions, they are rubbish at what they do! How can this be right? Nurse managers coming back, and newly qualified nurses trying to get appointments. It is so very wrong. I might even run for parliament and lobby that this be changed! I think it is just another example of how selfish this society, and individuals have become, '*Me, myself and I.*'

One aspect of music education I have little time for is self-aggrandizement or boasting. Music performance seems to attract a lot of this sort of people. From the word go in 1975, I have had both feet well and truly planted on the ground. My parents never pushed me into anything, and if I was happy, they were happy. I know that has never changed, and all too often I haven't been 'pushy' enough, but I will always be chivalrous to others where I can.

All too often in my musical career, I have come across divas and plonkers! (As I refer to them). I recall preparing to conduct a gala male voice choir concert, and the young male soloist, about 19 at the time, said to me, "you are honoured to have me here this evening, I turned down two gigs for this…" I just looked at him, in the '*Stephens' way,*' and retorted, "you, my friend, are the one who is honoured to be here this evening, performing with this choir, and certainly on my stage, with experience comes wisdom." I walked away, leaving him to catch his own chin as it dropped to the floor.

I came across these sorts everywhere, and usually teenagers who were instrumentalists as well as vocalists; the types where the parents (or should I say the mother) does all the talking, and it is brag, brag, brag from the outset. I switch off.

When I have given organ recitals, there is usually one or two people who approach me afterwards and say, "my son/daughter is an organist, and plays… blah, blah, blah." I think, 'right okay, and????' I couldn't care a monkey's throw if their son or daughter is an organist, good for them I say. Why tell me about somebody I don't know? It comes down to the simple fact they want to boast and brag. I have no time for it, but the more distinguished the musician, the less likely one is to have this sort of nonsense from them. It is worth pointing out here that my parents never praised me as a musician, or indeed an organist. They were modest beyond fault, and whenever praise was given, my father would say something like, 'I taught him all he knows,' and if I had a pound for every time I heard this. Another knock back was usually, "oh he didn't practice when he was small." This comment used to make my blood boil, as I was a long way from 'being small,' and I *did* practise, rather a lot, although thankfully it all came easy to me, so I didn't have to slog like many do. Oh no, my parents never offered me public praise at all, and they wouldn't now either. Not that I need it of course, I have always been satisfied with my own worth.

I have worked with several soloists at St David's Hall in Cardiff, where the word DIVA doesn't even cut it. They make outrageous demands of a certain flower in their dressing room, a certain type of bottled water, fruit, etc etc. Dear God! I have conducted in many venues and occupied No 1 dressing room. I don't expect anything other than an electric light to work! Why are these people like this? Not too sure really. Then you have the female opera singers who like to flaunt their magnificent bosom. We've all seen it on TV, and they come onto stage in the most uplifting evening dress you've ever seen and struts their stuff across the stage. The poor old men in the male voice choir almost suffer heart attacks there and then. A lot of these women know exactly what they are doing and love every second of it. I remember one such occasion in St David's Hall, Cardiff. I was occupying dressing room stage left 1, the premier dressing room I hasten to add. Terence Gilmore-James (Organist) in No 2, and next to him was a professional soprano, who shall remain nameless, but by heavens she had a huge ego!!

The afternoon rehearsal finished about 4.30pm, and always following a 3-hour massed rehearsal, I sit and reflect, alone in the dressing room, maybe going through the scores one final time. The soprano, two rooms down, was going up and down scales and arpeggios as if her life depended on it. So much so that Terence Gilmore rang me on the mobile from his room and said, "I wish she would grasp the song by now!" it was a funny moment, but when one is trying to relax, this sort of 'noise' can be most annoying, and many of these divas simply do this to be heard.

During the years that I taught, I had several pupils who never had any money, and there would be excuse after excuse as to why they didn't have it. They were delightful young people, and their parents were lovely, but they were poor, and any

167

conversation relating to money is very difficult to have. Despite the many excuses, I knew in my heart that they had little money and could not afford the lessons, but how could I deny these lovely young people the opportunity of learning the piano? It wasn't something I could sustain indefinitely, but for some time I turned a blind eye, and I taught them without any financial reward. Nothing was said, and no reference was made to it.

I cannot undertake engagements for no financial reward as Gail and I like a nice life, and that costs money, but we must all, from time to time in life, do a Christian deed. I hope that through this little gesture of goodwill that they appreciated the joy of learning a musical instrument, and I do hope that they look back with fondness.

I think all teachers will agree that most pupils learning an instrument do not carry it on beyond perhaps early teenage years. The musical ones do, but those who have been coerced into it do not, as there is no substance within them for the musical seeds to flourish and be nurtured. I have been very fortunate in so much that several pupils of mine went on to study Music at University, and some have become music teachers in comprehensive schools, and others are professional performers. It makes me proud to think that I was the person responsible for nurturing that musical seed within them, and with the encouragement of the parents, they succeeded in their musical studies. On the other side of the coin, you have teenagers who simply give it up when it is no longer considered 'cool' to be playing an instrument. Their ego and street-cred, need to be such that playing a musical instrument would be detrimental to their standing in their so-called society. It is a shame that there is sort of pressure on individuals to be like this, and we all can appreciate what it is like. I know more than most how much ridicule one gets when playing instruments, and I had added ridicule for going to church. Teenagers can be extremely cruel to each other, and you can be singled-out today for the slightest of things. Society has become sad, and it is a shame that there is such a marked decline in the number of youngsters learning a musical instrument, right across the country.

Also, there are new gimmicks on the market, such as 'learn online,' 'piano tuition online.' What poppycock! They are money making schemes pure and simple. The interaction between pupil and teacher, side by side, cannot be replicated when it comes to learning an instrument. I will never be convinced that this nonsense of learning a musical instrument 'online,' will ever bear fruit in the long term, *plus* it is doing music teachers out of a job.

In recent years I was also taught. I say recent, but I am going back to about 2003/4, when I applied to study part time at the Royal Welsh College of Music and Drama in Cardiff, where I wanted to study Voice (i.e singing). I went to the college to have my audition, and there was a panel there ready to judge whether I was worthy of a place in the college, albeit part-time. My accompanist was brilliant, and I remember the two 'contrasting' pieces I sang. The first was *'My little welsh home,'* and the second was *'Bella siccome un angelo'* from *Don Pasquale* by Donizetti.

169

I received the news shortly afterwards that I had been accepted to study voice with Mr Guy Harbottle and attended the college one day a week. It was a heavy commitment, but it was very rewarding. It was hard work, as I studied mostly operatic repertoire. I performed in some of the college musical soirees. It lasted 3 years, and by the end, travelling to Cardiff every week was somewhat draining. I was 33 years of age, and back as a student, with a student's ID card. The mind boggles! I was extremely successful, and although I had already had a degree of voice training as a chorister and learning from choirs that I had sung in as an adult, but this was very different and very challenging on the diaphragm. I remember in the next room to me was a Chinese student who was studying pianoforte. She was breathtakingly outstanding, and I would not have been worthy of turning her pages. She was on a par with the Chinese piano virtuosos *Lang Lang*. She made the most complicated Chopin prelude seem easy. Incredible talent. Very often we witness the Asian people as a race of immense talent, and this is not just about playing an instrument well, it is bringing playing to a whole new level. This is extreme ability combined with a tremendous gift, and usually it manifests itself when the individual is very young. They are certainly child phenomena and can gain very high musical examinations before their 10th birthday, which is simply mind-blowing.

## Chapter 12

*The Parish of Pembroke*
*&*
*The Parish of Haverfordwest*
*&*
*The Parish of Milford Haven*

After leaving St Peter's Goodwick in 1996, I spent some time undertaking freelance playing, and I was very busy, although it must be said, I was being asked to play everywhere for nothing. People often forget that musicians must eat! I had only met Gail the year before, and I wanted something of a 'normal' life too, but I guess you can take the man out of the church, but not the church out of the man, and I missed it.

I was reading the local newspaper in late 1996 and I saw an advert for an organist and director of music at St Mary's Church in Pembroke. I knew of the vicar, Revd Canon Colin Bowen, as he was a native of Tavernspite, and his father worked with mine, and his uncle was the cobbler in Whitland. I made contact and Gail and I went along to a service a week or so afterwards. I was hugely impressed, not only by the wonderful welcome we received, but of the musical standard on offer. The four-part choir sang beautifully, and the organ had a fine tone. I was intrigued. After some negotiating, I was appointed.

I worked hard to build on the already fine tradition at St Mary's Church. The choir, consisted of 4 trebles, 3 sopranos,

171

3 altos, 2 tenor and 2 bass. The balance was great, and they were a fine bunch. I introduced new anthems and canticles to them, and only a year after being there, the choir deputised for Cathedral choirs during their annual recesses. Such was their standard we could sing a full cathedral service and make a very good sound. We did have to 'recruit' some extras to do this, and two lovely people always jumped at the opportunity, Mr Ray Kane, who was an outstanding tenor, and Mrs Julie Orsman from Lamphey, who I learned, many years later, was the sister of my predecessor at Milford, Michael Nicholas.

Every year we sang Choral matins and Evensong at St Davids Cathedral, and Michael Slaney, MA FRCO., would accompany us. We also visited Llandaff Cathedral and Brecon Cathedral each year. We worked extremely hard in the lead up to such visits, and we would sing the traditional repertoire, an introit, psalm, anthem, canticles; all to an exceptionally high standard. I was very proud of them, and the adults of the choir were wonderful 'doers' and I must single out Mr Tom Pearce, who was head chorister. He really was the backbone of the choir.

In early 1997, when Gail was pregnant with our daughter, we went to St Mary's on a Saturday for me to prepare for the following day's service. There was a lovely lady preparing the altar flowers. She asked if I had keys to the vestry, which I did, and she subsequently left. Unbeknown to us, we were locked inside. I had keys, but for some very strange reason they would only work from the outside of the door!! A mobile phone had no signal inside, and we were stranded! Thankfully after much searching, I managed to get outside the church, but within the church walls, so were still not free. The only way out was climbing up a ladder and onto the vestry roof and sliding along that until we reached the main street. Then it was about a 10-15 foot drop down onto the pavement. There was no way that Gail could do this in her condition, and I also couldn't manage the drop into the main street from the vestry roof.

However, I put the ladder in place, and climbed up onto the roof, which was pitched. I slid along the roof very precariously, risking falling constantly! Eventually I arrived at the end of the vestry roof and looking down into the main street below. Thankfully, I judged a trustworthy individual correctly, and threw my keys to him, and he subsequently unlocked the vestry door, to be greeted by a very happy Gail.

News broke fast to the church folk, and the following morning at the service Gail had a large bunch of flowers for her distress. I can't remember what I had. Oh yes, nothing. I jest, of course.

I was very happy at Pembroke, and it was a busy and active parish. The choir even produced a CD! Which we recorded with Margarate Howells accompanying on the organ. Due to the position of St Mary's, right on the roadside, the traffic noise was prohibitive, so we recorded in our sister church of St Michael's at the opposite end of the main street. It was well back from the road, so an ideal venue. The CD sold like hot cakes, and even today I often play the CD, and it brings back some very happy memories.

One of the choristers lived in Sardis, so I used to pick her up every Sunday for service and drop her home afterwards. I enjoyed doing it as she was elderly, and I was passing the end of her road anyway, so it made some sense.

The travelling to and from Pembroke was a lot, especially for rehearsal which was sometimes twice weekly, and for services. I was only paid £10 per service back then, although the church provided me with pre-paid tickets to pay the cleddau bridge toll.

A few years passed and Colin Bowen was appointed Vicar of Haverfordwest, to be based primarily in St Martin's Church. For whatever reason, they were without an organist, and he asked me to go with him. For me, the only attraction was the lack of travelling involved as I was living in Haverfordwest at that time, and the church was renowned for a reasonable music tradition. I wasn't sure what to do, but in the end, I decided to take the opportunity. Throughout my life I have had to keep things fresh, and I don't believe in staying anywhere long enough to become stale, or to allow the experience to become stall either. However, now I am older, I am happy to meander down a gently-flowing stream, and as long as I can still gain some degree of inspiration, I am happy to continue, but it no longer has to rock my world as it were.

The people in Pembroke were really upset that I was leaving, but they understood the reasons. Like St Peter's Goodwick, I left on a happy understanding, and I knew that I was going to miss it. The parishioners were so lovely to Gail and I, and also after Jess was born they would love to have her in church.

Colin Bowen and I arrived at St Martin's within a couple of weeks of each other. I had not left Pembroke in the lurch because there were three organists that could take turns at helping, and Mrs Susan Jones was taking over as choir director.

St Martin's was a totally different kettle of fish, and I soon regretted leaving St Mary's Pembroke. The church was stiff and starchy, and the parishioners, except for one or two, were stinkers! They really did have a very high opinion of themselves and looked down on people who didn't attend St Martin's! There was also a couple of bossy women there who ruled the roost, one of which was a member of the church choir, and I grew to dislike her intensely.

I realised early on that I had made a huge error of judgement, but it was where I found myself, but it made me realise that grass is seldom greener on the other side. Revd Colin was hugely supportive and left me to the musical side of things, as there is nothing worse than a totally overbearing and interfering vicar! The choir would be very reticent to learn anything new, and they were so stuck in the past, it was soul destroying. There was always a big fuss made over the fact I had changed a hymn tune, and as for even thinking of a new anthem... forget it.

The atmosphere of the church was heavy and stale. Nobody was allowed to talk preservice, and as I say, everybody thought themselves superior. I say everybody, but that's not strictly true, because our long-standing family friend, Dianne Ball was churchwarden, and she was lovely. There was also a married couple who were both local GPs, and they were always hugely complimentary to me.

I managed to last 3 years before the situation became overbearing, and I lost interest. For me, as you will gather, once I lose interest in something it is an indication to me that it has reached the end of its usefulness, and this time had come at St Martin's. I spoke to Colin Bowen, and subsequently resigned. It wasn't terribly well received, and I worked a few Sundays as 'notice.' It's worth noting at this point that once notice has been served it is always best to go quickly. Working notice is of no benefit, and all too often relationships are then strained.

I left and found myself back on the freelance circuit. It was during this time that I joined the Cathedral choir as a bass lay clerk, as well as doing a lot of organ playing on a freelance basis. It was great, I was getting to do what I loved, being paid for it, and without getting involved with the politics that often exist. It was a role made in heaven.


Strangely enough, most of my freelance engagements were at St Mary's Church, Pembroke, where I had only come from 3 years before. They were 2 Sundays short a month, so after some negotiating on the fee of £25 per service, which I should point out is far less that the official RSCM rate of pay for somebody of my calibre, I began. It was good to be back as everybody was so friendly, and this time I didn't have the responsibility of managing the music, this was now being done by Susan Jones. I would accompany the choir for rehearsal and play on a Sunday morning, twice a month. It really was all I needed at that time. This arrangement lasted for some considerable time. My assistant organist at Pembroke was Anna Tiller, BA., who had studied music at Bath University, and was a former organ scholar at Bath abbey under Dr Peter King. She was an able player but lacked any confidence, but it was great to have somebody to fall back on. Anna was also my long-standing accompanist with Cantabilé.

After another couple of years, I was back at the organ of St Thomas' Church in Haverfordwest, playing at a wedding service of a pupil of mine, Christine Davies. It was a lovely day, and Gail and I were guests as we knew the family very well.
A week or so after the wedding, I received a telephone call from the curate of Haverfordwest, Revd Harri Williams. Harri and the then-vicar, Revd Paul Mackness wanted me to come to St Martin's vicarage one evening as they wanted my help. I agreed, and this was the first time I had met Fr Harri properly. I was immediately impressed with Harri's intellect and his ability to hold a conversation in the palm of his hand without any wooliness, and the straightforwardness of his manner appealed to me. I was told that Michael Grange, who was my successor at St Martin's had left, and they wanted me to come back.

I did say that I would only consider the offer if they agreed to pay me the same rate as I was getting on a freelance basis, and that somebody else be responsible for the management of the choir. Fr Harri, himself a musician and former Cathedral chorister, agreed to direct them himself, and I would accompany. With this in place, I agreed. My return to St Martin's was not a match made in heaven. One or two of the choir were very off-hand and distant and were still feeling let down from when I left previously. I was somewhat embarrassed about coming back I must admit, but I was assured by Fr Harri and Fr Paul that things had moved on for the better. They were both aware of the shortcomings of the church.

Sadly, Fr Harri couldn't keep his word about directing the choir, due to his workload, so I was lumbered with this once again, and nothing had changed. There was no willingness to learn new music, and Margaret Body was still as bossy and as controlling as ever. I did settle in, and to be fair it was a totally different experience as Fr Harri and Fr Paul had reformed the church, and people were more friendly than what they had once been. Revd Paul Mackness stood for no nonsense, and he was certainly brusque, although he and I got on famously together. He did possess a wicked sense of humour, and he was always very generous to me. It wasn't long after returning to the parish of Haverfordwest that I was appointed the director of music to the whole Parish – St Thomas' Church, St Mary's Church (on the hill), and St Martin's Church. This meant that I would be responsible for directing the parish choir, which was an amalgamation of the choirs from all three churches, and also, I would play the organ for any parish service. I enjoyed it and mixing with the other church people was lovely. Margaret Jones and Pat Swales from St Mary's and I had lots of fun. I recall directing the choir in St Mary's Church, and they were singing Mozart's *Ave Verum Corpus,* and it was somewhat 'rusty' shall we say. In fact, it was crap! However, it was a work in progress, and for the performance in a few weeks' time, I had every confidence that it would be fine. Margaret Jones, who was former Head of Music at Tasker

Milward school for girls was accompanying at the organ. A little bird flew into the church and was swooping up and down within the chancel and the nave, unnerving several the choir. After a time, the little bird flew into the chancel, between the choir stalls, landed upside down – dead! I stopped, and said, "Your singing is that bad, even the bird has committed suicide!" Everybody was in fits of laughter. It was happy times.

When Fr Harri left the parish to take up his first living at Milford Haven, the church was not the same. He brough a zeal, a presence, vim and vigour and this was no more. Fr Paul was not a people person, and soon church life started to lose its sparkle. Thomas Roberts, long-time server at St Martin's left to go with Fr Harri to Milford, as did some of the Sunday school.

A few months after Harri's departure, we welcomed the Revd Marcus Zipperlen and his family. Marcus was newly ordained, and this was his first curacy. A lovely chap who was extremely cool and calm. He was never going to be a Fr Harri.

Fr Paul was a member of so many diocesan committees that very often he would be away on a Sunday. On such occasions the retired clergy would make an appearance, usually in the form of Revd Graham Lloyd or Ven John Harvey. Fr Graham did a lot at St Martin's, and I worked with him a lot at Parc Gwyn too. The Ven John Harvey, former archdeacon of St Davids and rector of Tenby was something of a different character, and he was the person that brought about my final downfall from St Martin's. I must admit that I had once again made a mistake coming back, although Fr Harri and Fr Paul had changed much for the better it has to be said. One Sunday when Paul was away, the service was taken by John Harvey. The choir processed in to the voluntary, and as was customary, the hymn would begin when they had all arrived in the stalls. Today was going to be a different day. As soon as the choir were in the stalls, and I ended the voluntary, John Harvey spoke out, so the hymn was delayed. He said, "I can't believe Mr Organist that you have chosen such inappropriate hymns for today's service." I won't repeat in print what my first thoughts were, but safe to say that was my final time at St Martin's Church.

I was totally humiliated, and he had also embarrassed the whole choir and congregation with his outburst. I was as qualified to sit at the organ stool as he was to preach from the pulpit, and there was no way that he was going to get away with speaking to me like he did. My gut reaction was to walk out there and then, but this would have only caused further embarrassment to the choir and the congregation, so I thought better of it. Throughout the service I was angry and upset, and my mind had been made up. Many people approached me afterwards to offer words of apology on his behalf, bless them. The afternoon saw me go to the vicarage, and Fr Paul received my written resignation with immediate effect.

I must say that the church authorities did everything they could to try and persuade me to stay, but no, my mind was made up, and when my mind is made up there is no changing it. The time had come to go, and I owed it to myself not to be treated in this way. I vowed then that I would never darken the door of St Martin's Church again, and now, several years on I have not. On a slightly different note, I wonder how many of my readers believe in the paranormal?

In all the churches and cathedrals, I have worked at and been involved with, none of them have felt oppressive, but St Martin's in Haverfordwest was different. I've always had an ability to connect to my $6^{th}$ sense, and there were lots of strange goings on at St Martin's; I will tell you of two instances.

The first one was when I went to the church in the week, to sort some music in the vestry. I was only going to be a few minutes, so I left the main door to the church open, and I went up to the chancel and then into the vestry. I was only in there a minute or so when I heard the main church door slam shut. It was an almighty bang, so I immediately knew that somebody had slammed it because the inner main door is a long way through the porch, so wind would not have been a factor.

When I went to investigate, the door was in the same position that I had left it. This was very weird, and it did freak me out somewhat.

The second occasion was a few weeks later when I was in the choir vestry, which was located above the porch, accessible via a stone staircase. I was up in the little vestry room, and I could hear talking in the church. I heard them in the porch at the bottom of the stairs, and then go into the church. It was exactly at the time I was about to descend the staircase. The outer door of the church was locked after I came in, and when I came down the stairs, the door was locked exactly as I had left it, yet I could still hear talking inside the church. I couldn't make out what was being said but there was somebody talking, in

181

hushed whispers. I didn't like it one bit because how did they get in? I sheepishly crept into the church, and there was nobody there at all. I made a hasty escape I can tell you. There was no explanation for this, and I definitely heard talking, but there was nobody there. I have never felt such an oppressive atmosphere in any other church, and after this final incident, I never went into the church again alone.

After leaving St Martin's for the very final time, I was once again 'unemployed' as far as a residency was concerned but did some freelancing.

I missed going to church, so I decided that I would go along to Fr Harri's church in Milford Haven.

I had only been into St Katharine's church previously when I had accompanied the Landsker Singers on the organ. I was aware of the warm welcome almost immediately, and everybody was kind. Fr Harri came to chat as soon as he saw me, and it was good to see him again. He never referred to the fact I had left St Martin's, and neither did I.

The service was wonderful, and it was clear that he had worked his magic on the parish. The Sunday School was thriving, and I was impressed with the number of people that had turned out on a Sunday!! Well over 100 people in the congregation.

I had been going for a few weeks when Fr Harri asked if I would be prepared to join a rota of cantors for the psalm. I agreed, and every 3rd Sunday it was my turn. I enjoyed doing it, and had a quick run through with Mike Nicholas, the organist, before the service started. The other cantors were Fr Harri himself and his wife Clare. It wasn't terribly long after I started cantoring the psalms, that I joined the little choir. It was good to be back in the choir stalls again where it all started for me in 1975, and although the small choir was somewhat inconsequential in the grand scheme of things, they were a happy bunch who led the hymn singing best they could.

It wasn't long before the organist, Michael Nicholas asked if I wouldn't mind playing for the odd Sunday for him to have a rest. Here was a man in his 80s, so I was more than happy to help him out. I think it was two weeks later that I played, and I love it. The organ is a fine William Hill example, 1906, but fully electrified in 1988. It really is a joy to play.

Very sadly, Michael's health took a turn for the worst, and I had to play more and more. He was then hospitalized for many weeks, and his recuperation was long. To formalise the arrangement, I was appointed assistant organist. I suggested this to Fr Harri, simply because I didn't want anybody thinking that I was muscling in on Michael's domain and taking over. I would hate anybody to think this of me, and I have always resisted such instances.

However, Michael's health got worse, and I was playing constantly, week after week. I thoroughly enjoyed it, and it was a very enjoyable service. Fr Harri had theatre and drama in his worship, and this is something I love. It made you feel good, and certainly better for going.

In early 2016, Michael retired as Organist, and I was appointed Organist and Choirmaster. I was welcomed as one of the church family from the outset, and when Michael's health allowed, he and his lovely wife Paddy, sat in the congregation, and I always chatted with him. His favourite organ piece as the famous *Toccata and Fugue in D Minor* by J.S. Bach (BWV 565), and he would often ask me to play it, which I did, especially for him.

Sadly, Michael passed away in December 2019, and I missed our chats each week. He was a real gentleman, and somebody who always wanted to chat. Many people believe in some sort of divine intervention in our lives from time to time, and for me, I am wholly convinced that I was drawn to attend St Katharine's church after I left Haverfordwest for a purpose. These happenings seem to us mere happenings of the coincidental, but I believe there is more to it. It is all part of the mapped plan, and not only, by going there have I brought the church such gladness, it has fulfilled my career too. Oh yes, if we all stop and think about it there have been moments in life when some guiding hand was at play. I am wholly convinced that this is the case.

Our church family in St Katharine's and St Peter's suffered a huge blow in 2018 when Fr Harri and Clare left the parish to move to Walsingham in Norfolk. Harri informed me a few weeks before he made the public announcement, and I knew that it would never be the same again. We were losing a wonderful parish priest, with many gifts. He had recently gained his PhD., but he was always too modest, and played everything down. His final service was in November 2018, and on the 3rd of December 2018, several of us supported him at his installation in his new parish in Walsingham. I didn't go on the coach, as I went up on the day of the service, stayed overnight in King's Lynn, and then travelled home, via

Cambridge the following day, as I was calling at King's College.

We all missed Fr Harri dreadfully, and his faithful gathering of 100+ every Sunday without fail, soon started to dwindle away, which was very sad indeed. More bitter blows were to follow when we learned that the Parish of Milford Haven would cease to exist with the formation of a new Local Ministry Area, where 9 churches would be served by about 3 priests. It was ludicrous! Feelings ran high about it, and a church such as the Parish Church of Milford Haven deserved a priest all its own. Alas, despite much petitioning to the bishop, it did not come to pass.

I was asked by Milford Haven Junior school (Meads) to accompany the staff choir singing 'The Prayer,' for the final assembly taken by Fr Harri, who was also chair of governors. Very unfortunately I could not attend on the day, but my recording of the accompaniment, and having worked with the staff choir for some weeks prior, it worked well, and everybody was so grateful. I was even very kindly given a nice bottle of vino for my effort!

The new LMA was formed, and Fr Andrew Johnston was appointed the 'priest in charge,' which was a new concept for me.

It took a good deal of adjustment, and we still miss the style of Fr Harri in 2021, and I guess we always will. To add insult to injury the Corona Virus pandemic hit hard in 2020, reducing our congregation further, and the church was totally closed for 3 months. We are now averaging about 30 on a Sunday. I do hope that some will return when we get back to some sort of normality. At the time of writing, May 2021, we are still not allowed to sing. The choir has not met in over a year, although I now play pre and post music and something incidental during the service. It's not the same, but I'm hoping that we will be back to some form of normality soon. We have recently acquired a brand-new set of Hymn books in memory of a faithful member, but we cannot use them.

I am ever so grateful to many of the parishioners who have always been so kind to me, and so very complimentary about my organ playing and choice of music. I must single out Mrs Dorothy Hickson, who often chats to me about the music, and to have some words of thanks and encouragement go a long way, even to a seasoned old fart like me. Mrs Sonia Dudley and Mrs Pam Fisher are also forever contacting me as a way of thanks. This is all so much appreciated. I have made some great friends at St Katharine and St Peter's Church, none more so than Mrs Vivienne Barrat and Mr Davy Rowland, Mr and Mrs Ralph Potter, Mr and Mrs Frank Ashton, Mrs Primrose Griffiths, Mrs Elizabeth Bearne, Mrs Annelise Tucker and her family, and so the list goes on. In fact, everybody is so lovely there, and I do hope and pray that our numbers will increase once again.

At the time of writing, we are awaiting a new curate, Revd Hannah Karparty. I remember Hannah being a teenager in school, and I remember with much fondness her parents Martin and Barbara, when Martin was the rector of Monkton, and during my time in Pembroke, I worked closely with him.

When I was in Pembroke, I was also editor of the deanery magazine, *The Bridge,* and would spend one Saturday every month, along with Steve Johnson from St Michael's photocopying, stapling and distributing, so Revd Martin Cox and I became good friends. I remember our many conversations about Hannah, being a typical teenager, and here I am, now waiting to welcome her into our midst as an ordinand, a new assistant curate. It really is a very small world. Martin is currently the rector of Narberth, having returned to this diocese from Swansea and Brecon as vicar of Gorseinon.

St Katharine and St Peter's congregation is, in the main part, opposed to ordination of women to the priesthood, and these wishes must be respected. However, I am of the belief that God, through the Holy Spirit has guided Hannah to us to bring new growth, facilitate new faith and to perhaps build us back up to where we once enjoyed. I like to keep an open mind, because I know some very able and fine female vicars, many of whom are delightful.

Although I have now played in churches for 41 years, I still look forward to doing it. I still get a buzz of excitement each time I play. Funnily enough, if it is a special service, or something out of the ordinary, I do get a little anxious now, and I guess this is perhaps my age. It is very slight, but it is helping to keep me on my toes.

I love St Katharine's and St Peter's and the people that go there. I have no intention of leaving there, and as long as the church does not close, it is my intention to retire from there, after completing hopefully 60 years of playing.

## Chapter 13
*Haverfordwest Male Voice Choir*

In 2010 I was appointed Musical Director of the renowned Haverfordwest Male Voice Choir. I had associations with the choir many years ago, in 1991 to be precise, when I was their assistant accompanist, when D Gwyn Griffiths was MD, who had a reputation of being a tyrant, and that reputation was spot on!

When I took over in 2010, my predecessor was Christine Shewry, and somewhat a déjà vu, as she was the MD of Whitland Male Choir before I took them over too. She had worked her magic here again and hammered the choir into the ground. Morale was non-existent, and the standard of the choir was poor. When I say poor, to the untrained ear they would sound perfect, but their diction, vowels, consonants, and diphthongs were way off. I had my work cut out, and I had been pre-warned by the committee as to what I was in for.

I took a slowly, slowly approach, but I have always been a conductor who praises a choir, and never humiliates anybody. It was a philosophy that worked, and soon I had the choir loving their rehearsals again, and they were eating from the palm of my hand. Unfortunately, the accompanist, Carys Evans was due to finish her role as she was moving to live in Ireland, so for the first month or so, I was the accompanist *and* conductor, which is difficult! We met each week on a Friday in St Martin's Church and community Hall, but our rehearsal moved to a Monday evening, with an 8pm start to ensure that those members who were farmers could get there.

I raised the standard of the choir to somewhere that it had never been at before, and they could stand shoulder to shoulder with any male voice choir in the country.

Rehearsals were now attracting 50 plus members, and everybody was loving what they were doing. I would start every rehearsal with a 'sing,' warts and all, and just allow them to sing through. Afterwards we would work incredibly hard until 9.45pm, and the last 15 minutes would also be some good sings, usually hymns with large a-mens, which is synonymous with male voice choir repertoire. My teaching technique with choirs is legendary, and it enabled the male choir to learn between 11 and 17 new pieces per year, and copy free at concerts, which is one hell of an achievement. I don't believe in a lot of wasting time by 'note-bashing,' and the piano playing everything before each section sings. The accompanist will play the introduction and the first note, and then we give it a go. Mistakes don't matter, and polish is the very latter stages of learning any piece. This method has always brought me success, and it makes for a confident choir. The choir took part in 3 or 4 massed concerts at the Royal Albert Hall during my tenure, and the conductor of the festival, Dr Alwyn Humphreys *always* singled out the Haverfordwest choir at rehearsals as the only choir that knew all their work. This was a great accolade, and one which the choir were greatly proud of, and they had much respect for me and what I was bringing to the choir.

In January 2011, Peter Griffiths was appointed accompanist. Peter lived in Milford Haven and has never driven, so it was agreed that I pick him up and take him home every week. It was a commitment, but Peter was a great accompanist and very loyal to both me and the choir. Peter and I worked extremely well together, and we knew how each other worked, which was always a key to success. Peter was a confident accompanist, and I could always rely on his ability. When he did get it wrong, like we all do, I always ignored it unless it impacted on the choir greatly. Far too many conductors belittle their accompanists and I detest it. Having been an accompanist myself, I know what it is like when the conductor has a very big ego and relishes every opportunity to make an accompanist look foolish.

I remember many years ago when a conductor asked me at Ysgol y Preseli (where I was rehearsing with a choir) if I could play the piece. I retorted, 'don't you worry about my playing it, I'm more concerned as to whether you can conduct it or not.' That comment brought the house down, and it certainly put the conductor in his place.

During my time with Haverfordwest choir we gave some wonderful concerts, and I will always remember them with great fondness. One of my favourite times with the choir was a weekend spent in Barnstaple with their male voice choir, singing at their annual concert. It was a wonderful weekend of music, fun, and fellowship. I conducted some of the concert and was organ accompanist for some too. I also recall singing at St Chad's in Shrewsbury; we had a brilliant day. The choir were always very responsive to my direction, and they never let me down. I remember singing in London for a wedding of a member's son, and once again it was sublime. The registrar took exception that we were singing a piece with religious overtones. In fact, it had two words in it that reflected biblical text. She was really rude to me about this, so she had one of my specials, and I 'dressed her down,' severely, and it is safe to say that the choir *did* sing the song as intended.

The downside of the choir, although thankfully there were not many, was that the committee could be very short-sighted when it came to future proofing the choir, or for moving forward in general. I did try to bring in some infinitives, but they would always find a reason as to why it couldn't work. As I have said earlier, I am a very optimistic individual whose glass is always half full, and I often came against negativity from some of the more miserable members shall we say.

One such occasion was when a trip to our twin town of Oberkirch in Germany was arranged. In fact, I was town councillor at the time, so it was doubly important for the choir to make a good impression.

The chairman at that time was Colin Hancock, who is around my age, and to be fair to him, he wanted to move the choir forward into the future too. Sadly, because the choir had travelled numerous times to Oberkirch since the formation of the twinning some 25 years earlier, many of the members were moaning that they wouldn't come because they had been before. I supported the chairman whose view was that many members have not been before, and as a team it was the responsibility of everybody to participate.

Unfortunately, only 26 choristers committed to the trip out of 53, which was very disappointing, especially as it was my first trip abroad with the choir, although we had been to the Isle of Wight (if that counts!). Peter, our accompanist couldn't come as he was already committed to his role with Neyland Ladies' Choir who were going to Spain at the same time. Thankfully, former principal accompanist Wendy Lewis, ALCM., agreed to come with the choir. Wendy and I worked well together, although she was a very unconfident player; I think she was frightened of me for some reason. The concerts we performed in Oberkirch were brilliant. Thankfully the vocal balance of the choir was just right, and we 'knocked 'em dead' as the saying goes. I was a very happy MD! Over the years we made great friends with the Sepp Ganter Band, which is a carnival band in Oberkirch. As you may know, Germany is famed for its wind bands, and the Sepp Ganter is one of their best. I made some great friends in the band, and we keep in touch.

We were also invited to Australia but sadly the choir membership was just too old to make this trip, so we had to decline.

It doesn't matter how talented or qualified a conductor is, if you have not got a good committee running the affairs then you are on a hiding to nothing. Success also depends on who is the chair of the committee, and this varied greatly over my 8 years with the choir. Some chairs were very good, and others only promoted their own self-interests, and were not encouraging to members. I won't name anybody individually, but one chair was very much a welsh nationalist, and did not give our English friends a very warm welcome. During a particular chair's term of office, he wanted me to select a programme of 80% welsh. This was not doable in my opinion, and we had several disagreements over this. Some chairs always think they are right, and this one was such. I couldn't believe that farmers were telling me how to manage a choir! As I said earlier, I value opinions, but I also value them greater if the person dispensing their opinion knows something about what they are saying. All too often in the choir they did not.

Like most male choirs in Wales, membership is ageing, and it is increasingly difficult to recruit new, young members. The generation of today are not interested in joining a group of men who are seen as *Dad's Army*. It certainly wouldn't be a 'cool' option for some youngsters to consider joining a male choir. Haverfordwest Male Voice Choir was founded in 1896, and this is an incredible heritage, of which they were justifiably proud. I also felt very honoured to have been part of this musical history and legacy within the town.

Whilst recruitment was a problem, retention was even more difficult. The existing members, comfortable with each other, were not the best at welcoming and mentoring new members, and all too often the newbie would be fending for himself. It is a very lonely experience walking into an established group, and certainly not for the faint hearted. Sadly, many came along but they never came back. I quite accept that it is not for everybody, the commitment is enormous, and membership can be very expensive.

One very good top tenor member, Revd Arfon Thomas made a connection for us with his father, a very eminent conductor in Bath. He tried in vain for us to team up with some choirs in the Bath area, and I am convinced that because the chair at the time didn't like Arfon, therefore it never materialised. Sadly, Arfon left the choir, and he cited the fact to me that it was directly due to the attitude of the chairman. In fact, the attitude of the chairman cost us the membership of 6 young members, who were good singers, and had been with the choir several years. This was a very heavy blow for the choir, and a step too far in my opinion.

During my time as MD, I founded the choir patron scheme which raised over £7,000 for choir funds, and we had well over 100 patrons. It was a great success story, but it was always something that many resisted, simply because the MD is 'ex-officio,' and they felt that I should not be doing an active committee role. How short sighted this was, but I ploughed on regardless.

Each year in the autumn, the choir held their annual celebrity concert in the hall of Sir Thomas Picton School. These were superb concerts that always attracted between 600 and 700 audience numbers. Over the years we had names such as Wynne Evans, Sian Cothi and others as our soloists.

In 2018, my granddaughter was born, and I guess this changed my life considerably. This was not an easy time in our lives as the birth were not straightforward for our daughter and we could so easily have lost both through hospital neglect, but that's another story and battle that I just stopped fighting last year!

I'm not sure exactly what happened but I lost my 'mojo' for the choir, and I soon found it had become a chore to go along.

This was my issue, not the choir, and I felt bad for it, but I was where I was, and other things had to take priority in my thinking. I guess I was somewhat mentally exhausted and tired.

In the autumn of 2017, my friend and colleague Mr Huw Tregelles-Williams, OBE MA DL FRCO., agreed to accompany the choir on a hired organ for our annual concert, following a very successful concert a month earlier in St Davids Cathedral where Huw accompanied us on the organ there. I managed to persuade the choir to hire a digital pipe organ for the cost of £1,000. This was a small cost when charging £15 for a ticket and they sold 700! The concert, which again attracted a sell-out audience was an outstanding success, and many comments said that it was the 'best yet,' to which I will agree. The boys were on a high and the afterglow in the Hotel Mariners in Haverfordwest was second to none.

A couple of weeks later, the sub-committee, who was responsible for the organising of the annual concert met up, and it was agreed that we do a repeat performance and ask Huw again. The decision had to be ratified by the executive committee, but this was, as far as we were all concerned, a rubber-stamping exercise. Sadly, it turned out to be anything but, and they refused. They said that if I wanted an 'organ sound,' then Peter could press the 'organ' button on their electric keyboard. This just goes to show how much they know. This goes to show how much these farmers knew about quality music and managing a quality concert. They showed no regard to my years of knowledge and experience, and I felt it was a slight to Huw Tregelles, who was, after all, President of the Welsh Association of Male choirs. In fact, I was embarrassed by their decision. Sadly, I felt in my bones that Peter Griffiths was at the bottom of this decision because he didn't like Huw and held him in little regard, and I had doubts as to anybody else thinking about this possibility. In fact, dear reader, Huw is one of the finest organists in Great Britain, having been Head of Music at the BBC for many years, and having played all over the world.

It was this that extinguished my love for carrying on as musical director. I felt that all the work I had done over 8 years, and they were happy to undo it all and regress.

I also felt betrayed by Peter, and here was another example of somebody who I considered a friend going behind my back to assassinate the personality of Huw Tregelles-Williams. It was so uncalled for and a manifestation of pure old jealousy!


I knew what was for me because that light of love had been extinguished, and when this happens, I know it is time to move on. It's the story of my life and has always happened. I cannot change it, I cannot fight it, and it is what makes me me!

However, I did not want to make a hasty decision, and I knew deep down I would miss the choir if I walked away. I had invested so much energy and talent into the choir that to walk away would be throwing it down the drain. I thought of nothing else, and in the end, I requested a leave of absence, which was granted.

My leave of absence was a time that I used to reflect and to really think about what I wanted to do and where my future lay.

My health was also deteriorating, and I found myself not having the vim and vigour as much as I did and coupled with the thinking that one must always quit when ahead, my decision was reached. I was not to return to the choir. In my heart I was not convinced that I was making the right decision, but there was no other option. For me it had turned stale and sour, and I simply did not have the energy to work my magic again. The time had come to move on.

It was also at a time when the tenors were really struggling, and some concerts they were only 2 in the section, which was not a feasible option long term. All these things I factored into my decision. I also had to look after my reputation, and I will explain what I mean. If a conductor stands in front a mediocre choir, then he or she is seen in a poor light, of not being very good, and I was not prepared for the choir to do this to me when the opposite was true. This might be slightly self-centred of me but in my defence, I am fiercely proud of what I have achieved over many years of hard slog, and nobody is going to take that away from me, choir or individual.

I resigned as MD of the choir in December 2018, and I do miss it. We had some great times, and they were good fun, and it was the only choir which I can honestly say I felt held in high regard, but I guess all good things must end. I will always remember the wonderful concerts we had, especially those with the Hywel boys and girl singers from Llanelli under the direction of John Hywel Williams, MBE., I also recall a wonderful concert in St Davids Cathedral with Gwawr Edwards and Catrin Finch (Harp). They are memories I shall treasure. Some 3 years on I still miss the great camaraderie that existed in the choir, and I must say that male choirs have the best camaraderie out of any group. Members are close knit and very proud of the badge that is emblazoned on their jacket. They were happy times, and I do miss being part of it. Perhaps I was too hasty, but I do believe that there is a natural end to anything, and this was it.

## Chapter 14
*Bits and bobs...*

This rather short chapter, towards the end of the book, is a purposed addition about 'this and that,' or as the chapter is entitled, 'bits and bobs.' I guess it is about little bits that cannot really be put into any other chapter.

Back in 1984 (or thereabouts) I became involved with the Whitland Pantomime association. It was a group formed by the late Jean Jenkins and Kaye Shrivelle, who had moved to Whitland from the smoke. I went along, first of all to be in the chorus, and I found out quite early on that I enjoyed it. Many of my school friends were in the association, and I knew everybody in the cast too. Nobody was a stranger, so it was great. Even the vicar Nigel Griffin played the role of 'Buttons' in Cinderella, which was the first pantomime we ever staged. What fun we had, and the ad-lib and inuendo by the late Maisey Skyrme and Gwyneth 'knackers,' made them a huge hit. I ought to point out at this juncture that Gwyneth was called 'knackers,' due to having some connection with the slaughterhouse in Whitland. She was a scream! We performed the pantomime to sell-out audiences for 5 nights in a row, and it was a lovely time. When I was 16, I became secretary of the association, and I enjoyed 2 years in that role. I have always been able to write a good letter, so I did enjoy the administration side of the association. They were happy times and I have very fond memories of my time with the pantomime.

As I said earlier, I am not a sporty person, but I did enjoy playing bowls. In fact, I played for the Whitland team when I lived at home, and I even competed in the meads' sports centre in Milford Haven. Whitland Church had a men's fellowship team, and I was involved with that too. Sadly nowadays, I couldn't play bowls due to the arthritis in my hips, but I always enjoy watching it. There is nothing more relaxing than watching a game of bowls live.

I promised you earlier in the book to tell you a little bit more about the antics of my friend Colin Rogers. Colin was a brilliant stage craft marshal, and I engaged him in every massed choral concert I was involved with. There was nobody else that could even come close. Colin was a perfectionist beyond measure, and he would never compromise. To hear him bark and bawl at the ladies' choirs from South Wales, and they often retorting back was very funny. He was receiving as good as what he was giving.

I just want to share one tale with you from a massed male choir concert that I conducted in Cardiff, and of course Colin was the stage manager. He had planned the allocation of dressing rooms over 5 levels to the choirs, and the rooms were greatly varying in size, so he allocated them according to the numbers of members as supplied by the choirs in advance.
He would ask if any members were slightly infirm or on walking sticks, because they would be in the green room off stage right.

## Dream, Believe, Achieve

When it came to the stage rehearsal in the afternoon, he was poised on the rostrum, his both index fingers poised to be dropped to give the visual signal to start the 'parade.'
The tiers were filled nicely, and everybody did what was expected of them, and then in came to fill stage platform last. Unbeknown to Colin there was a disabled member confined to a wheelchair. When he gave the signal for platform entry, this very enthusiastic man came in his wheelchair, speedily shoving the medal wheel rim between his hands, tyres squeaking as he went. Colin immediately blew his whistle and called everything to a halt. I remember the words well, "what is that contraption?" The man stopped dead in his tracks, or on his wheels, and said, "I'm disabled," to which Colin replied, "that's all very well, but I cannot have you leading in so fast, go back and come in slowly."

The gentleman had to spin round and go back as did all the other men. Colin was satisfied that they were ready again, and dropped his fingers for them to file in. The man in the wheelchair was so slow, it was like watching him move in slow motion. "Hurry up, push your wheels faster!" colin was doing the mimicking of pushing the wheels either side of him. It was funny I have to say, although it certainly was not 'PC.'
The man in the wheelchair couldn't get it right to suit Colin, so in the end he was banished to the farthest end and last to enter.

The chairman of the choir objected to Colin saying that this chap was not visible from the auditorium, and this was his first concert, and as such his family were coming to the performance to support him, and such they wanted to see him. I couldn't believe what Colin said next. "This is a concert where you will all perform together as a team, there is no room here for individuals. If his family wishes to see him all evening, bring a photograph!"

I couldn't believe my ears, and whilst I wanted to laugh, I thought it best not to. Colin had no problem with saying anything. The stage was his as far as he was concerned, and he took no nonsense from anybody, and certainly he knew what to throw at them verbally. When the men were all in position, he pulled a tin of Kiwi boot polish from his pocket and held it high. "Do you know what this is?" he bellowed. Obviously, they answered yes, to which he replied, "make sure you bloody use it then!"

Then he walked off stage and came back on carrying an ironing board and iron, shouting the same thing. "Make sure, these are bloody used tonight, I want everybody to be pins in paper." It was very funny to be fair and when one of the men voiced his opinion that was at odds with Colin's opinion, he barked, "when I want your opinion, I will give it to you!"

I had never heard that expression before, and it is something I have adopted. I thought it funny. Colin was not somebody who was impressed with status or the standing of anybody, and he treated everybody the same. I recall Lord Ellis Thomas having a photo call with us on stage, following a dress rehearsal, and he was speaking when he wasn't supposed to be, so the next voice to be heard was Colin's, as he tore him off a strip. He told him that he might well be presiding officer in the assembly, but on *this* stage, Colin was in charge, and he was to do exactly as he was told. Colin told him that opinions are not important to him unless they were his own. I knew Colin well, and I knew how to handle him. We got along very well indeed, and I took little notice of his nonsense to be fair.

Colin and I had been friends since 1990, and he was a member of Haverfordwest Male choir when I was their MD. Colin always believed he had a good solo voice, which wasn't strictly the case. He asked me to give him a solo spot in a concert, and one such request was overheard by the chairman, and at a subsequent meeting of the committee, his request was discussed. The committee felt most strongly that Colin is not permitted to sing with the choir as a soloist. I just stalled Colin and avoided the subject as there was no way I could hurt his feelings in this way. Very sadly, in the end, he thought it was my doing, and he stopped talking to me. He resigned from the choir, and I never heard from him again. I heard in 2019 that Colin had died, and I will always regret not telling him the truth of what happened. My loyalty ought to have been to my friend and not to the committee of the choir, and this was a very poor lack of judgment. Colin and I worked extremely well together, and I will always be very grateful for his expertise on the stage. He had a wonderful sense of humour and how we laughed over the years. He was a very generous man, and he was so happy with his better half, Joyce. He found happiness with her in his autumn years, and they were well suited. He was also a very good and experienced chef, and his meals were second to none. No expense would be spared in getting the best possible steak, and always washed down with an expensive wine. He really knew how to host a great experience.

RIP old friend, and I have no doubt that you are putting everybody in their place up in that great concert hall in the sky, and if you are not, you should be! Go easy on Gwyn Griffiths, he knew no better!!

## Chapter 15
*The Future...*

Wouldn't it be truly wonderful if we could predict the future? I suppose in a way we can – death! This is the only certainty we will ever have in life; we all come in the same way, and we will all go out the same way. The bit in between is made up of good fortune possibly, hard work most certainly, and much disappointment too. When we get to 50 years of age plus, we begin to start thinking about our own mortality, especially as we see contemporaries starting to fall off the mortal coil. It can be, and often is, very sobering. I don't fear death, as my Christian faith gives me hope and surety of better to come, but I do fear the journey. I do fear the way out as it were, but this is not in our control, so que sera sera.

On a more tangible topic, the future of music, arts and church music is something that puts fear into my heart. Community choirs see their membership ageing with very few youngsters coming into the ranks, so eventually these wonderful organisations will cease to exist. The average age of a male voice choir is worryingly high, and whilst some of the choirs have the odd young member, it is the **odd** too. Again, the future is limited for them, I guess. The same is true of any organisation that has only now got an adult membership.

As for churches, chapels and organised religion, there is no guaranteed future. Secularism in this world is forcing these wonderful places to close at a rate of knots. If one travels through the south Wales valleys, as an example, the number of chapels, that were once thriving, heart beats of a community lie idle, empty, dusty, and falling down, unless they have been metamorphosised into a boxing club or night club, or with increasing popularity, a dwelling. Who would want a lovely home surrounded by a graveyard? It really is sad when you see such wonderful heritage rotting into the ground and being consumed by nature. These places were once resounding to great hymn singing and indeed the centre of the town or village, they were a way of life. Nonconformist movement was prominent in Wales, and many of the preachers were 'brim and firestone,' and everybody would be thrown into hell for not going to chapel. The ministers were really revered, and the nation was a God-fearing people. I always think that if pews in such places could talk what a tale they would tell. Generations of faithful worshippers sitting on them week after week, listening to the word and trying to live their lives in a good way, or at least being 'seen' to be. They were good days, and it is a shame that our heritage has, in so many places, been relegated to the history books.

Music as a subject in our schools is becoming something of an 'inferior' subject. Funding for the arts is decreasing faster and faster, year on year. The music service for schools is wholly inadequate, with students only receiving a small amount of time per lesson, which always must be supplemented by private tuition. We focus far too much on these so-called 'core subjects.' Mathematics and a science etc. Okay, in normal, everyday life, one needs to know how to add, subtract, divide and multiply. Unless a career requires stupid study of all that specialised mathematics, who needs it? The limit of my mathematical knowledge was sufficient to understand music and its timing etc and note values. Other than this, I use the lovely calculator on my iphone.

Music and other expressive arts ARE essential and SHOULD be a core subject. Individuals who are successful in Music are usually highly bright, and intelligent individuals and extremely academical. Music is not an easy option, it is one of the most complicated subjects in the curriculum, and to master an instrument to near perfection takes a huge commitment and ability. I remember an old teacher who said to me, "no good learning an instrument if the child is thick, won't get anywhere!" Whilst this statement would kill one of the 'PC do gooders,' it is, in essence true, so it annoys me when educationalists and their ill-advisors belittle the importance of Music and the arts in our schools and spend all their time and energy in promoting sport, Mathematics and Science. I could, of course go on and on about something I am passionate about, and I love to orate. People seem to forget that I had a measured IQ of 148 and have achieved 9 sets of 'cap and gown,' qualifications, so with that comes an active mind, a questioning nature like none other, and I am not one to sit back and allow mushy-brained people tell me how it is. I appreciate that this may sound slightly arrogant, but I must be true to myself in everything I do. I don't suffer fools gladly, and believe it or not, there is still a lot of them out there in society – most of them seem to cross my path daily! I'm not overly competitive, but I don't take failure lightly. Failure to me is catastrophic and needs to be avoided at all costs, and when I do fail, I beat myself up about it for weeks. There is no need for failure, one should have prepared sufficient well to avoid it in any given situation, and I know that people say to me, 'you tried your best,' but when it comes to any personal failure of mine, this just doesn't cut it.

This country is becoming a greedy, selfish, and secular one. Murders are now so common we barely ruffle our feathers when we learn of one. If a black man is ruffed up, the world goes berserk, but when the white woman is killed by a rapist, very little is said. We fly the rainbow flag of inclusivity at every opportunity, but why not also fly a flag for the family unit, for the mother's union? Why not fly a flag promoting the nurturing properties of a loving family of mum, dad and 2.4 children? There are a lot of good deeds being done in this world, but they are blinded by the evil which exists in the hooded gangs that roam our streets, and society must stand back and allow it to happen. Minority groups now rule supreme, just to satisfy the need for political correctness in this country. People will protest at the drop of a hat, and an opinion cannot be voiced because it will probably cause offence to somebody.

What is so wrong with the values of the past? Human decency, manners, politeness, care for each other, and the list could go on. Nowadays we dial for our food and goods,

without leaving our armchairs, we have 10,000 channels of 'tosh' on the television, the internet is bursting with indecency and pornography of every description. Why?

Why is there a need for this? Drugs are now more popular in our schools than learning, and there are more sales of drugs in our comprehensive schools than on the streets. Why? Usually, to get to a definitive answer we need to ask the five why's, but we could ask ten and I don't think we would get a satisfactory answer.

Domestic abuse is on the increase, genderless identification is causing boys and girls not to know whether they are Arthur, Martha, or a teapot! The Gingerbread Man has turned into a 'Gingerbread *person,'* and we cannot say 'Boy and Girl,' in schools now, as it could cause offence, if one doesn't 'identify' as such.

I really would love to meet the despicable idiot who thought this tomfoolery up. I'm sorry to say that flogging would be too good for the clown. Unless somebody (or the vast majority) of society 'grows a set of balls' and stands up to be counted, then down the swanee river we will go, into some sort of oblivion, and everything we have held dear will go with it.

As you can clearly see, I have no faith in this country having a decent future. I fear greatly for my grandchildren's future, and we have most definitely had the best years up to this point. In addition to being a musician, I am also a historian, having gained BA (Hons) in modern History and the past teaches us so much, and what our forefathers did for us ought to remain uppermost in society's ideologies. I'm not a man of modernism, I am a man of tradition. It's about hitting the right balance. My motto is 'As modern as tomorrow, but with a lot of time for yesterday.'

As you now know, in 2020 I celebrated 40 years as a church organist. Will I make it to 50 years? I know full well at some point my church, like all the others, will close. It will cease to exist **unless** something radical happens and the youth have a vision. If society continues to plummet down the pan of secularism, such places will not be needed. The word of God will be irrelevant in the lives of... probably, everybody!! I don't like looking at anything from a cynical perspective, but is it a realistic perspective? Even if places of worship survive, will LIVE music within them survive, or am I to be replaced with a CD? Where are our future organists coming from? Musical tradition in worship is something that I will fight for. As many of you know, I love modern, sacred songs, but I do not subscribe to some of the modern forms of delivery, but that is just because I was brought up as you have read. I would love to think that I will still be playing the organ in church when I am 80, having clocked up 70 years of playing in church, but it is very unlikely. If our current youth attendance is anything to go by, there will be a congregation of 3 or 4 each week, hardly sufficient to sustain a church. I shudder to think, and it saddens me greatly. If I was given a wish, it would be for a return to a time when churches were flourishing, and respect for everything and everybody was uppermost in people's minds. Even now for funerals, I am replaced by recorded music, although I will fight the fact if this is the start of a slippery slope.

So, dear friends, I have almost come to the end of this little musical journey of mine. As I said in the beginning, it was no way exhaustive, but rather some snippets to give you a little insight into what makes this flesh and blood tick. I hope you have enjoyed the read, and always remember that there cannot be an ending, it is just where we leave the story. The story of us all will continue, into the future, when we ourselves become memories, we will still be thought of (hopefully). Do your bit now to make this world a better place for us all; do your bit to maintain the moral fibre of this country; do your bit to bring back innocence to childhood, and do pray that there will be, someday, a return to all things that we cherished dearly.

I would hate to think of church and sacred music being a thing of the past and indeed organists being a thing of the past. Are we relevant in today's society? Even if there are signs of growth, it can be nurtured for future generations.

Modern thinking and modern ways are all very well, and in many cases, it is well justified and beneficial, but there is still a lot of mileage in traditional, live music in churches, accompanied by the organ. As much as I love modern sacred songs, I am not a lover of guitars in worship as I was not brought up that way. Of course, it works for some people, and this is great, but I hope and pray that within the desire to create a 'modern approach,' our church authorities down get sucked into a false sense of security of modernism and resort of cinema screens, and 'funky news for modern man', woman, or teapot!! Let's hold dear to what our forefathers worked hard for, and the generations of loved ones gone before us. This is not too much to ask I don't think. It saddens me sometimes to think that my musical involvement is in a dying art, because I wonder what is the future for church organ playing? Oh, I often hear it said that I could 'diversify,' but at 51 years of age I don't really want to. Musical enjoyment and fulfilment aren't the same as it used to be I don't think, because society is changing, and there is not the philosophy anymore for what I have held dear all my life. Our churches have changed to be seen to be inclusive and the scriptures have changed to make the text more modern and appealing... what? It really is a wonder that the Lord's Prayer has not changed to "Our mother..." I will always be a man of principal, and as I said earlier in the book, I will remain at St Katharine and St Peter's Church until I retire (God willing) or it closes, whichever is sooner, but I will not stay if the church authorities decide to marry same sex couples in a place of worship. This to my belief would be a step to far, and something I would not want to be part of. Hopefully, common sense and the word of God in the Bible will prevail. We have had sufficient 'funky news' to last a lifetime. I really do wish that time could be wound back 30 years' plus, to a time when humankind was far more gracious to each other, and there was a mutual respect, and of course a much greater love of Music too!!!

## Chapter 13
*.... And finally*

I have reached my final chapter, and this is probably more of a summary rather than anything else. I have been hugely fortunate in life to have been blessed with such a wonderful gift and talent. My path was, I believe strongly, mapped out for me, as it is for all of us, perhaps even before we make an appearance in this world, but this is something we will never know, or perhaps we will when we reach the eternal kingdom.

Within the last 12 months, since the start of COVID-19 lockdown, I have entertained many people on my electric Yamaha Clavinova, by hosting *'Friday night is music night'* on social media, LIVE. I began by recording videos of my playing musical theatre and other contemporary repertoire, and then I decided to give LIVE feeds a go. It was an instant hit, and so successful that I didn't look back. My *'Friday night is music night'* has reached people in Australia, New Zealand, Canada, Germany, France as well as the United States. I received a lovely message from an elderly lady who lives in Atlanta, Georgia. She married a Welshman, and music was his passion too. What I was playing reminded her of him, and she looked forward so much to listening to me. Because of the time differences between our two countries, she never listened LIVE, but when somebody is 4,290 miles away and takes the time get in touch, I know that I have done something right. It is such a privilege to know that what I do is bringing enjoyment to people, and this is a wonderful thing to be able to do. On the other side of the coin I have had some messages from pretty strange people too, mostly from Africa I should say, but I guess they were false facebook accounts just waiting to hack me, thankfully to no avail. My PC and informatics system has more security than Fort Knox.

My musical nights on the piano, at their peak have attracted 125 viewers, which is incredible. As time went on, numbers dropped a little, but at the height of the lockdown, people were looking forward to having my music as their company on a Friday evening.
In addition to a Friday evening, on a Sunday evening I hosted a LIVE feed called, *'Sacred songs @ 7.'* This hour or so of sacred and classical music was aimed at a niche audience, particularly those who were regular church or chapel attendees, and they were currently denied the opportunity to music in their places of worship.

I play modern sacred songs as well as traditional hymns, and classical piano music by the great masters, all of which is wonderfully received. I look forward to these LIVE feeds, and my audience has become a regular group of people. I wish there was more, but I cannot force people to watch me, and of course, not everybody likes music darling! During these evenings, I have received wonderful feedback from people I have never met, but I feel that I now know them. The lovely family of Norma Lee, her daughters Yvette and Lesley, and granddaughter Alice; and Catherine, Paul and Lucy-Evelyn Beddowes; Vivienne Barratt and Davy Rowland and my sister-in-law Pammy, and of course Mum and Dad. These lovely people have hardly ever missed a single 'show,' and I have grown to know many new people over that time. There are lots of people from the south Wales valleys who tune in on a regular basis, and the interaction between people is delightful. I am overwhelmed by the love that is out there for *my* music and long may it continue. The summer months may see numbers tumbling, but I am going to keep this entertainment source going until such time I don't manage to attract an audience, or numbers drop so low that it's no longer worth my effort.

For me, music must **always** be about enjoyment. Little else matters, and we must always do what we enjoy. Life is too short and fragile to do anything under pressure, or to continue doing something if we find it a chore. Throughout my career I have lived to this philosophy. I have never allowed any appointment to become stale, boring and tedious. I always know when it does and when the time is right to move on. Not everybody will share this view, but as I have always said, and will continue to say, *know when your sell-by date* has expired and allow new blood to pick up the torch to carry it forward. I suppose it could be regarded as something of a regret that I have allowed my impatience to get the better of me, especially in my younger, less mature years. If I become disillusioned or cease to enjoy something, I walk away and leave it behind. I just cannot continue to do something that does not inspire me, and I know that over the years I have let organisations down, simply by being true to my philosophies. I also believe that with age comes wisdom, and when I think back to the early 90s, I see a different person to what I am now. With experience comes wisdom, and nothing can be a substitute. As we mature, we become wiser, or at least that's the theory! Musicians are, as I said earlier, a peculiar breed and we are very exacting people. We are hugely sensitive and don't tolerate any second-rate performance or experience, and in such instances, fuses can be blown. I can say, hand on heart, that I have never 'blown a fuse,' *if* my singers or pupils are putting in an effort. If individuals are making a good, concerted effort then I am happy.

**Always** do what makes you, and your nearest and dearest happy. For all the commitment one shows to organisations etc, as soon as you have gone, you become a memory all too soon. As I said earlier, people are loyal to their *need* of you, and not loyal to you as an individual, and how I have found this out over the years. Human nature and behaviour can be very demoralising, but we must try to dust ourselves off and carry on.

I cannot look back and harbour regret as it will not achieve anything, but I do have some small regrets, but nothing I can do now will change the course of history, so we learn to live with it, and move on. I hope that what I have done musically, and perhaps in public roles, will be remembered with fondness, and that the pupils I have taught, will always spare a thought when they get older and maybe take a stroll down memory lane. All of us leave a legacy, and if I can leave a legacy which is a smile, then I will have achieved what I set out to. I also hope that choirs I have directed will remember a tolerant man who always had their best interests at heart, and the numerous accompanists I have worked with, remember a gracious director. I *always* give praise because it is very important and negativity is detrimental to the soul, and it can have a very significant effect on people. I have always, without exception, put enjoyment into *everything* musical I have ever done, and made individuals feel special about themselves. I have never belittled anybody in Music, but I build them up to be the best that they can be, and I want to use what skill and gift I must instil in performers what I was lucky enough to have instilled in me. It is important to realise that *everybody* has feelings, and it is far too easy, especially in today's society, to hurt these feelings. One day we will face judgement, so it is very important to live the best life we can in the best way that we can whilst here on this mortal coil.

As we get older, our memories become even more precious. Memories are little treasures that we keep locked in our hearts forever, and music is a great facilitator, and will instantly evoke a memory, a place, memory of loved ones no longer with us; such is its power. Music is so powerful that we all take it for granted. I must pinch myself very often when I am seated at the organ, playing for a large service, simply taking it in my stride. I forget that I was given a truly wonderful gift and I have done everything to nurture it along a sometimes-arduous path. My teachers had faith in me, my parents, grandparents, and great aunt had faith in me, and so did very many individuals that I have met on life's journey. I always go out of my way to encourage music's new blood, and it warms my heart to see and hear young people on social media, playing their instrument or singing, and when I witness this, I become encouraged that music is still very much alive, and long may it be so.

*Dream, Believe, Achieve*

As I head into 2021, my only musical commitment is to my lovely church of St Katharine and St Peter's in Milford Haven. I am extremely happy there, among such lovely people. Never say never, and if the right opportunity came along for me to dust off my DJ and baton, I will be on it like a 'good 'un' as they say in Pembrokeshire lingo, but I will also be very choosy because to take on the wrong, or inappropriate project would result in me becoming dejected, and then having to walk away because it has become stale and unfulfilling.

As I mentioned at the very start, this book is but a very small bit of my musical life and career, and I have selected bits and pieces, so the 'story' isn't too tedious, and I also had to think about the cost of its production! I reckon to give you the full, unabridged story would expand the book to 1,000 pages, at least!

Thank you so very much for reading but a small part of my career to date, and I want to thank all those truly wonderful and special people who have made the journey so worthwhile, especially my dear wife and soul mate, Gail. This wonderful woman changed my life and changed me for the better, and no thanks will ever be enough for that.

2020 was a great 40th year anniversary for me, and I was very fortunate to have been the recipient of some very prestigious honours. I became a Fellow of the National Federation of Church Music (FNFCM) in recognition of my achievements in church music over 40 years. I was also honoured with the AFNCollM – which is an associate Fellow of the National

College of Music and arts, London. I was also admitted into the Guild of Musicians and Singers as a Fellow (FGMS), which is a learned society in London. In 2021 I was truly honoured to become a Fellow of the National College of Music and Arts, London (Hon.FNCM) which was conferred on me for my 'outstanding contribution to music and the arts.' I am in such company as the organist of Notre Dame and many luminaries in the world of professional music. It makes me extremely proud to be recognised in this way. The MBE would now finish it off nicely LOL. One award that has alluded me sadly, is the archbishop of Wales' award in Church Music (AWACM) which I would dearly have loved to gain, but alas it was not to be. I have yet more plans to keep sitting examinations at the highest level as it will keep the grey matter working.

In June 2020, I became an Honorific Lord following the acquiring of some land which is part of the ancient estate of Hougan in Cumbria, which was highlighted in the Dooms Day book. This has appealed to my historical side, and although owning a very small piece of history is good, the legitimate and legal entitlement to be known as 'Lord' really is the icing on the cake, and I will use it on occasion, especially when we want the best table at a restaurant or seats in a theatre! Well, if you got it, flaunt it!

I hope the legacy I leave is that I brought lovely music to many people and made a difference to their lives.

*Dream, Believe, Achieve*

Always remember what I have said…. **There is no end, it is just where *we* leave the story……**

# The End

Richard Stephens, BA (Hons) Hon. FNCM.,
FVCM (Hons) AFNColl.M. FNFCM. FGSM.FSCO. CTVCM.
MNCM. ANCM. AVCM(Hons) ARCM.FRSA.,

***Organist, Pianist, Conductor, Teacher.***

*"Music is the language of the soul and the key to our innermost thoughts."*

*Dream, Believe, Achieve*

*Pictured at the organ of Barnstaple Parish church, when I
accompanied the Barnstaple Choir at their annual concert*

*Dream, Believe, Achieve*

*At the organ of St Katharine and St Peter's Church*
*Milford Haven, where I am*
*Organist and Director of Music. 2016 -*

*Pictured at the organ of St Peter's Church, Carmarthen*
*following an organ recital in 2014*
*I was organ scholar at St Peter's between 1986-1988*